KV-510-484

Peter Hepplewhite is an escaped history teacher, currently hiding in the Tyne and Wear Archives Service, where he works as Education Officer. He has been a freelance writer for more than ten years, starting with school textbooks before he realized that war stories were more thrilling.

Neil Tonge is a successful children's author steeped in a love of history. His books cover a wide range of subjects that appeal to all ages.

Also from Macmillan

WAR: STORIES OF CONFLICT

Compiled by Michael Morpurgo and featuring
brand-new stories from Joan Aiken, Eva Ibbotson,
Jamila Gavin, Elizabeth Laird, George Layton,
Geraldine McCaughrean, Margaret Mahy,
Michelle Magorian, Michael Morpurgo, Eleanor Updale,
Celia Rees and other top children's authors.

THE WORLD OF ANNE FRANK

Compiled by The Anne Frank House

MALKA

Mirjam Pressler

WORLD WAR II
IN ACTION

PETER HEPPLEWHITE and NEIL TONGE

Illustrations and maps by David Wyatt

WESTERN ISLES
LIBRARIES

30575242J

J940.53

MACMILLAN CHILDREN'S BOOKS

First published as *A World in Flames: World War II In the Air*
and *A World in Flames: World War II On Land* 2001
by Macmillan Children's Books

This edition published 2005 by Macmillan Children's Books
a division of Macmillan Publishers Limited
20 New Wharf Road, London N1 9RR
Basingstoke and Oxford
www.panmacmillan.com

Associated companies throughout the world

ISBN 0 330 43438 1

Text copyright © Peter Hepplewhite and Neil Tonge 2001
Illustrations copyright © David Wyatt 2001

The right of Peter Hepplewhite and Neil Tonge to be identified as the
authors of this work has been asserted by them in accordance
with the Copyright, Designs and Patents Act 1988.

All rights reserved. No part of this publication may be
reproduced, stored in or introduced into a retrieval system, or
transmitted, in any form, or by any means (electronic, mechanical,
photocopying, recording or otherwise) without the prior written
permission of the publisher. Any person who does any unauthorized
act in relation to this publication may be liable to criminal prosecution
and civil claims for damages.

1 3 5 7 9 8 6 4 2

A CIP catalogue record for this book is available from the British Library.

Printed and bound by Mackays of Chatham plc, Chatham, Kent.

This book is sold subject to the condition that it shall not,
by way of trade or otherwise, be lent, resold, hired out,
or otherwise circulated without the publisher's prior consent
in any form of binding or cover other than that in
which it is published and without a similar condition including
this condition being imposed on the subsequent purchaser.

CONTENTS

CONTENTS

WORLD WAR II IN THE AIR

PETER HEPPLEWHITE

To Addy, the aerial baby

In 1998 newspapers carried a strange report. A 71-year-old man drove his car into a ditch because he thought a passing plane was about 'to shoot him up'. A few weeks earlier he had suffered a terrifying nightmare for the first time. He was running headlong from German fighters that dived at him with guns blazing. And, as if that wasn't bad enough, when he tried to get away, he was pursued by a pack of fierce dogs.

Night after night the same terrible dream recurred and he woke sweating and exhausted. The only thing that would calm his mind was visiting a quiet field where he could hear the voices of long-dead friends. What on earth was happening to him? Slowly he told a psychiatrist his story.

The man was a veteran of World War II. He had watched German air raids pound British cities in the first few years of the war while he was a teenager, and made up his mind to strike back. When he was 18 he joined RAF Bomber Command and went on to fly 30 missions over Germany. In many of these he watched helplessly as other members of his crew were killed by enemy fighters or anti-aircraft fire.

On his last mission in December 1944 he parachuted from a burning plane and was captured by the Germans. Four months later he escaped, only to be hunted down by guards with dogs. For years he coped with the memories without too much difficulty – then suddenly they became too much to bear. Fifty years after World War II ended he was suffering from battle shock. He was still paying the price of the war in the air.

Many of this veteran's experiences were shared by over a million men and women who served in the RAF during the war. Those still alive are now in their late 70s or older. Their memories of events are mixed. The war was a time of achievement, friendship and excitement but also of sadness, death and destruction.

This book snapshots six stunning stories from that whirlwind time and gives you the fighting facts behind them.

- In 1940 Stuka dive-bombers pound a Sussex radar station. Will they blind Britain's electronic eyes and pave the way for a German invasion?
- As the Battle of Britain reaches its height a desperate Hurricane pilot runs out of ammunition. How

can he stop a German bomber heading straight for Buckingham Palace?

- Deadly Focke-Wulf fighters pounce on a Lancaster bomber over Berlin. Does the stricken plane stand a chance of ever making it home?

- Trapped by searing anti-aircraft fire, an American B-17 bomber bursts into flames. Will the courage of one crewman be enough to fight the fire?

- Blowing down the walls of Amiens prison and rescuing 700 Resistance fighters. Is this a mission impossible for the Mosquito squadrons?

- During the summer of 1944 a new weapon blasts London. Can Britain's best fighter pilots stop the sinister V1 flying bombs?

RADAR
WARNING

BATTLE BRIEFING

No Surrender

By the end of June 1940 German forces had conquered most of Western Europe. The British army had been defeated in France and had barely escaped from the wreckage-strewn beaches of Dunkirk. As the summer drew on Adolf Hitler, the German leader, expected the British to negotiate peace – that seemed the only sensible thing for them to do. But the British didn't see it that way. They rallied around their maverick Prime Minister, Winston Churchill, and fought on.

The Battle of Britain

On 16 July Hitler signed the order for Operation Sea Lion, the plan to invade southern England. But before the German army could cross the Channel, the Luftwaffe (the German air force) had to snatch control of the skies and wipe out the Royal Navy. In their way stood RAF Fighter Command. Churchill called this epic struggle for survival, 'the Battle of Britain'.

On Sunday 18 August, 1940, the Germans launched an air raid to punch a hole in Britain's radar network (see Fighting Facts) and 24-year-old WAAF (Women's Auxiliary Air Force) Corporal Joan Avis Hearn found herself in the front line ...

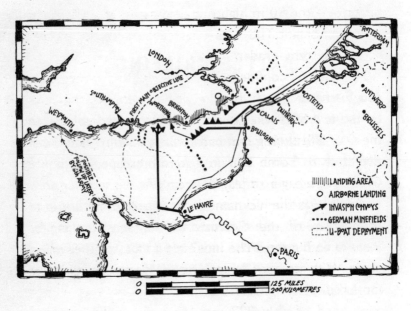

The plan for Operation Sea Lion.

THE STUKAS STRIKE

Dive-bombers

The Stukas were lined up proudly, ready for take-off. Thirty-two-year-old Major Helmut Bode was to lead the attack. He was in command of the 31 planes of Third Group, Dive Bomber Geschwader 77. Their target that afternoon was the 'radio station' at Poling, near Littlehampton in Sussex. He had not been told their true purpose – the 90 m high metal masts were, in fact, far more important. They were part of Britain's top-secret defence system – radar.

Helmut was confident. He knew the RAF would be a tough nut to crack, but he had no doubts that the Luftwaffe would win. Stukas had been the spearhead of the Nazi **Blitzkrieg** that had conquered Europe. Now it was time to bomb Britain into submission and Third Group were eager to play their part.

'Stuka' was the nickname for the Junkers 87, a shortened form of the German word for dive-bomber, Sturzkampfflugzeug. The Junkers was a strange-looking plane. With its bent wings and fixed undercarriage, it looked like a prehistoric bird. It was slow too, with a top speed of only 232 mph. But the Stuka was not designed to take on enemy fighters. It was a deadly precision bomber. Each aircraft was loaded with a 250 kg bomb under the **fuselage** and four 50 kg bombs under the wings. When the Stuka began its screaming dive, few targets survived intact.

At 12:30 exactly, Helmut opened his throttle wide and bumped across the grass airfield near Cherbourg. Fully laden, his plane lumbered slowly into the air. Poling was only 85 miles away, about 30 minutes' flying time. By 12:45 the rest of the Group was airborne and in formation around him. And they were not alone. Three other Stuka Groups, assigned to knock out coastal airfields, soon pulled alongside – a grand total of 111 dive-bombers. Minutes later, this air armada was complete, as an escort of around 55 Messerschmitt Bf 109 fighters swung into position above them. Helmut had the comforting thought that any Hurricanes or Spitfires that tried to interfere would get a rough reception.

Time to Duck

At Poling radar station, Joan Avis Hearn had gone on duty at 13:00. Joan was one of the first women to train as a radar operator and had been posted to Poling in December 1939. Radar was still top-secret and she had been warned not to talk about her work. She later recalled:

> The local people probably thought that our two tall radar masts – one for transmitting and one for receiving – were some kind of science fiction 'death ray'.

Service life for Joan had been a strange mixture of luxury and rough-and-tumble. Since there were no

WAAF Corporal Joan Avis Hearn.

RAF barracks at Poling, the WAAFs stayed at Arundel Castle. They shared a suite of rooms, with their own butler to serve them meals. In contrast, the station was little more than a series of wooden huts protected by sandbags. A new, blast-proof concrete bunker was almost finished but by the summer of 1940 only the telephone links had been moved into its protecting walls.

Shortly after Joan began her afternoon watch it

Aerial view of Dover.

became clear trouble was brewing. The Poling radar screens showed a big raid building up over France – Helmut Bode's Stukas! When Joan was ordered into the bunker to operate the telephone switchboard, she had a feeling of dread. Nearby stations at Rye, Pevensey and Ventnor had been bombed in previous days. Was it Poling's turn now she wondered.

Joan didn't have time to worry for long. Soon she was busy passing radar plots of enemy planes from Poling and other nearby stations to the Filter Room at Bentley Priory. There should have been two WAAFs handling the flow of calls but the station was shorthanded and she struggled on alone.

Suddenly at around 13:30, Sergeant Blundell rang through with an urgent message. 'Raiders, Joan! Time to duck.'

'Sorry, sir,' she replied, 'I can't leave yet, there's too much information coming in.'

Moments later an urgent voice came over the line from the nearby radar station at Truleigh Hill. 'Poling! Poling! Do you realize the last plot we've given you is right on top of you?'

And even as Joan listened, an eerie sound drowned out the warning – the scream of dive-bombers.

Stuka Attack

Four thousand metres overhead Helmut Bode dropped his Stuka into an 80-degree dive, fixing his sights on the target buildings.

At 485 kph he plunged 3,000 metres in less than 30 seconds. As he dropped he sprayed the radar station with machine-gun bullets. Woe betide any defenders who didn't keep their heads down.

At 1,000 metres a warning horn sounded – four seconds to bomb release.

At 700 metres the horn cut off and Helmut hit the release button on his control column.

As the bombs fell away an automatic pull-out system heaved the nose of the Stuka level with the horizon. The crushing return of gravity smashed him back, hard against his seat. On either side of Helmut two other Stukas went

Stukas diving to attack.

through the same drill at the same time. It was a unit ploy, always strike in threes to divide the fire of anti-aircraft guns. In less than five minutes the attack was over and Third Group were streaming back to France.

Tiny Heroine

At only four feet ten inches tall, Joan Avis Hearn was the smallest recruit in the RAF, but that afternoon she was to show the courage of a giant. As the dive-bombers screeched and bombs burst round the bunker, she pulled on a tin hat and stayed at her post. She believed that any information she got through to Bentley Priory might be vital in repelling the attack.

In the midst of the explosions a shocked and shaken Post Office engineer staggered in. It was his unlucky day. He had been installing new telephone lines when the raid began. Joan didn't show him much sympathy, however. She thrust a receiver into his hand and ordered, 'Repeat everything I say to you.'

Calmly Joan continued to read the plots from other radar stations while her reluctant ally passed the messages on. At the other end of the line, the Filter Room plotter could hear the bombs raining down. Her anxious questions echoed over the receiver. 'Poling, Poling, are you all right?'

For a short time the brave pair battled on, then the explosions came too close. A near-miss ripped the blast-proof door off its iron hinges and the telephone switchboard went berserk, with lights popping and bells ringing. Through clouds of dust and debris an officer burst in and ordered them to get out quickly. Joan emerged into a scene of chaos. Bode's Stukas had dropped over 80 bombs. Half of them had hit the station. She remembered a scene of devastation:

> There were craters everywhere, the concrete aerial supports pitted by machine-gun bullets and the top of one of the masts shorn away. The lorry that brought us to Poling that morning was burning fiercely, and the officer's lovely Lagonda sports car was a gutted wreck. Our only defence was a Lewis gun (machine-gun) manned by an army detachment whose billet was a mass of flames.

On reflection the arrival of the Post Office engineer probably saved my life. If he hadn't turned up, I might have been tempted to run for it. I wouldn't have stood a chance ...

Counting the Cost

On the way home Helmut Bode's pilots escaped lightly. RAF Hurricanes and Spitfires pounced but only one Stuka was shot down, while a second crash-landed in France. Their comrades were not so fortunate. Other units had been harder hit, especially First Group during their attack on Thorny Island airfield. The **Luftwaffe War Diaries** later counted the cost:

Of its 28 aircraft twelve failed to return and six others were so shot up that they only just made it back to France. Adding the casualties of the other Groups, 30 Junkers 87s were either lost or severely damaged. The price was too high.

After this bruising day, Stukas were considered too vulnerable to face RAF fighters. They were not used in large numbers again during the Battle of Britain.

In spite of the destruction Joan had seen at Poling, the radar station was only partly damaged. The long-range radar was out of action until the end of August, but the system for detecting low-flying aircraft was quickly in action again. Mobile transmitters were set up in caravans in the nearby Angmering woods and only two days later picked up the plots of another large raid.

Still nervous, Joan was delighted to see the German formations smashed by the RAF before they got close. The Luftwaffe had failed to wreck Britain's invisible shield.

On 22 March 1941, Joan Avis Hearn was awarded the Military Medal by King George VI at Buckingham Palace. When the King asked about her work, she carefully replied that she was a telephone operator. After all, radar was hush-hush and no one had told her if His Majesty knew about it. If he didn't, she wasn't going to let the cat out of the bag.

FIGHTING FACTS

The Winning Formula

German Plans: The Luftwaffe had to gain 'air superiority' (control of the air) over southern England so that the German invasion fleet could cross the Channel safely.

Objective 1

Bomb targets such as airfields and factories to force the RAF to protect them with Spitfires and Hurricanes. Catch and destroy these modern fighters, leaving Britain without air defence.

Objective 2

With the British fighters out of the way, use bombers to sink the Royal Navy.

The Luftwaffe wanted Fighter Command to slug it out for command of the air, like two heavy-weight boxers – winner takes all!

Order from Herman Goering, Commander-in-Chief of the Luftwaffe, 19 August, 1940: *Inflict the utmost possible damage on enemy fighter forces.*

British Plans: The Head of Fighter Command was Air Chief Marshal, Sir Hugh Dowding. He realized that to win the battle of Britain his force of some 700 Hurricane and Spitfire planes had to hold out against over 1,500 German bombers and 1,100 fighters. Winning did not mean destroying the Luftwaffe but making sure enough fighters survived to protect the Royal Navy – and make a German invasion too risky.

Order from Air Vice-Marshall Keith Park, Commander of No. 11 Group, 19 August 1940: *Our main object is to engage enemy bombers.*

Radar Evens the Odds
If the RAF knew how many enemy planes were coming – and if they could attack them at the right place, the right time and the right height – their chances of winning would be much greater. Fortunately, from 1936, Dowding had backed a high-tech defence system that gave exactly this information – radar.

Death Ray Experiments

Have passing planes ever caused interference on your radio – just when that crucial goal of the match is about to be scored the sound is drowned by static? When radio broadcasts began in the 1920s it was noticed that signals were often disrupted by aircraft. This led to some wild ideas:

Wild Idea 1

Electromagnetic waves might kill the aircrew of enemy planes – a death ray.

Wild Idea 2

High-powered radio waves might be used to detonate bombs on board an enemy aircraft before it reached its target.

Weird! But interesting enough for the Air Ministry to pay for more research. In 1935 Robert Watson-Watt, head of Radio Research at the National Physical Laboratory, investigated and dismissed these theories as science fiction. However he did have a practical idea:

Common-sense Idea

Watson-Watt proved that radio waves could be used to detect aircraft by measuring the time it took for a signal to bounce back from a plane. It was the start of four years of hectic work.

By 1939 the east coast of Britain was guarded by two radar systems:

1. the Chain Home stations that detected planes 100 miles away, and
2. the Chain Home Low stations that located aircraft flying under 1,000 m.

Chain home radar towers.

Radar Control

Both radar systems fed their information by telephone to the Filter Room at Fighter Command Headquarters at Bentley Priory, in Middlesex. The Filter Room was a telephone exchange where the information was collated and cross-checked before it was sent to the Operations

The filter room at RAF Fighter Command Headquarters, Bentley Priory.

Room. Here a giant map and 'ops' table displayed aircraft tracks over the whole of Britain and the sea approaches. This gave Dowding and his commanders a complete picture of each day's battles.

The British 'Few'

On 20 August 1940 Winston Churchill praised the pilots of Fighter Command and called them 'the few' who 'are turning the tide of war'. Although they were only a tiny part of a huge war effort by tens of thousands of people, the Battle of Britain was won by the skill and courage of 3,080 pilots. Sadly, 515 of these were killed. Although the majority were British, many airmen of different nationalities also served – and almost 100 of them died.

Fighter Command – The Few

Nationality	Number of Pilots	Number Killed
British	2,543	478
Polish	147	30
New Zealand	101	14
Canadian	94	20
Czech	87	8
Belgian	29	6
South African	22	9
Australian	22	9
French	14	0
Irish	10	1
American	7	1
Southern Rhodesian	2	0
Jamaican	1	0
Palestinian	1	0
Total	**3,080**	**515**

The German 'Few'

The Luftwaffe Messerschmitt (Me) 109 fighter pilots could not be blamed if they also thought of themselves as 'the few'. Certainly, if bombers are included, the

Main German aircraft in the Battle of Britain

Type	Max. Speed	Range	Weapons	Comment
Messerschmitt 109E, single-engined fighter. Nicknamed the 'Emil'.	357 mph (576 kph) at 12,300 ft (3,750 m)	410 miles (660 km)	Twin machine-guns in the fuselage and two 20 mm cannon in the wings.	The equal of the Spitfire and armed with cannon.
Messerschmitt 110, twin-engined fighter. Nicknamed 'the destroyer'.	336 mph (541 kph) at 19,685 ft (6,000 m)	565 miles (910 km) Able to reach almost all of England and Wales from northern France.	Two 20 mm cannon and four small calibre machine-guns.	One of the best twin-engined fighters in the world, but no match for Hurricanes or Spitfires.
Junkers Ju 87 'Stuka', dive-bomber.	238 mph (380 kph) with bomb load at 13,410 ft (4,085 m)	370 miles (595 km)	Three machine-guns, two firing forwards, one backwards. Bomb load of about 500 kg.	A very accurate bomber but slow and vulnerable to fighters
Junkers Ju 88, twin-engined bomber.	224 mph (448 kph) with bomb load at 18,050 ft (5,055 m)	1,055 miles (1,700 km) with extra fuel tank.	Four hand-held machine-guns. Bomb load of 2,000 kg.	Good as either a horizontal or a dive-bomber.
Dornier Do17, twin-engined bomber. Nicknamed the 'flying pencil'.	224 mph (360 kph) with bomb load at 13,120 ft	720 miles (1,160 km) with bomb load and extra fuel tank.	Four hand-held machine-guns. Bomb load of 1,000 kg.	The Dornier's air-cooled engines were less vulnerable to enemy fire.
Heinkel He IIIP, twin-engined bomber.	247 mph (395 kph) with bomb load at 16,400 ft (5,000 m)	1,224 miles (1,960 km) with bomb load and extra fuel tank.	Five to seven machine-guns. Bomb load of 2,000 kg.	The most numerous German bomber during the Battle of Britain but also the most vulnerable.

attacking German air force greatly outnumbered Fighter Command. But the most important fighting was between Hurricanes, Spitfires and Me 109s.

At the beginning of the Battle of Britain the Luftwaffe had about 725 109s ready for action – almost the same number of fast, single-engined fighters as the RAF. On 1 September this number had fallen to 438 and by 1 October to 275.

WAAFs at War

The Women's Auxiliary Air Force was set up in June 1939. At the time of the Battle of Britain women were limited to half a dozen RAF trades, including cooks, drivers, telephonists and barrage balloon fabric repairers. And then there were the clerks (special duty) – a boring name which hid front-line action during the summer of 1940. These were the women who manned the ops rooms, radio interception stations and radar stations – women like Joan.

Listening to the Enemy

One of the best-kept secrets of the war was the 'Y (Interception) Service'. WAAFs who could speak German monitored radio transmissions, and by listening carefully to the 'chatter' of German pilots were able to build up a picture of the Luftwaffe Order of Battle – a detailed list of the units attacking Britain and where they were based. Horribly, they also listened to the sound of

WAAF recruiting poster.

men dying in their planes. Section Officer Aileen Morris remembered:

There were occasions when we would intercept a message from a German formation approaching RAF fighters ... having spotted our aircraft before they themselves were observed. We were then likely to hear: Indianer unten fuenf Uhr, Kirchturm 4, Aufpassen *(Bandits below at five o'clock, height 5,000 m, look out). In those days we were unable to get through in time for it to be of use, and would get hopping mad that we had no means of warning our fighters that they were about to be jumped.*

Then Angreifen (attack) the formation leader would yell, and we would know that the German fighters were diving on their target. I would hear one of the RAF monitors murmuring: 'Oh God ... oh God ... please ... please ... look up ...' and I knew how helpless she felt.

There was sympathy too for the Germans. A WAAF sergeant at Hawkinge airfield in Kent was used to hearing a cheery-sounding Luftwaffe pilot as he made regular reconnaissance trips over the Channel. Then, one day, he was shot down in flames by Spitfires. She recalled:

He was unable to get out and we listened to him as he screamed and screamed for his mother and cursed Hitler. I found myself praying, 'Get out, bale out, oh please, dear God, get him out.' But it was no use. We heard him all the way down until he fell below reception range. I went out and was sick.

The Battle Goes On
The day of the attack on Poling saw the hardest fighting in the Battle of Britain. The Luftwaffe lost 71 planes and the RAF 27. But the struggle was far from over. The make or break day for the Luftwaffe was to be 15

September – remembered since as Battle of Britain Day. As you will see in the next tense chapter, Hurricane pilot Ray Holmes was in the thick of the action.

BATTLE OF BRITAIN DAY

BATTLE BRIEFING

The Blitz Begins

On 7 September 1940 the Luftwaffe began raids on London. This was the start of the Blitz – 76 nights of non-stop terror bombing. During this first attack German bombers escaped almost unscathed. RAF flight controllers had mistakenly sent their fighters to protect airfields to the north and east of the capital. It would not happen again. In the days that followed the Luftwaffe paid a heavy price.

On 15 September radar reported the largest German formations yet seen heading for London. The twelve Hurricanes of 504 Squadron, based at RAF Hendon, were among the fighters waiting for them ...

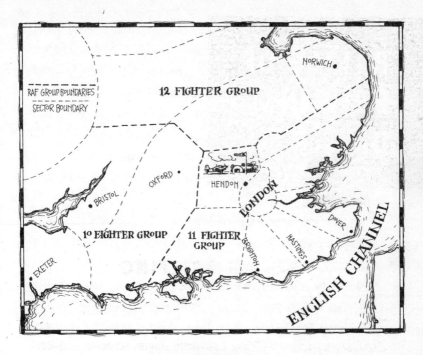

Location of RAF Hendon.

SAVE THE PALACE

A Long Morning

Sergeant Ray T. Holmes, 'Arty' to his mates, sighed as he stepped into a hot bath. 'What a maddening time it has been,' he thought crossly as he looked at his watch. 'Almost 11 o'clock. Where are the Luftwaffe? What is going on? We've been ready for take-off since sun-up.' As he lay back and began to relax, his mind flicked back over the events of that trying morning.

It had begun with the usual early start. At 05:00, still in darkness, Arty and the other pilots of 504 Squadron had stumbled out of bed and dressed. Still bleary-eyed they had climbed into the Humber truck, that carried them to their planes. While they were driven round the airfield perimeter track the usual rude banter began.

'Own up, who peed in my shoe last night?'

'Sorry, old chap, I couldn't wait. You know how far the toilet is.'

'It's not good enough, pee in your own damn shoe.'

'Well, if you feel like that about it I'll use someone else's ...'

Nobody minded that this was the same silly prattle they had heard yesterday ... and the day before ... and every day since they had been stationed at Hendon. When death was peering over their shoulders, laughter was precious.

By the time they arrived at **dispersal** they were awake and chirpy. It was just as well. The next job was the careful inspection of their planes and equipment. It was the same vital routine every dawn.

CHECK: helmet, parachute and map.
CHECK: fuel, guns and radio.
CHECK: engines, hydraulics and electrics.

When he fought the enemy at 300 mph (480 kph), 15,000 feet (4,570 m) above the ground, the last thing Arty wanted was a blunder that should have been spotted on the ground. His ground crew were superb, but it was comforting to know he had looked over things himself.

With the inspections finished the commanding officer (CO) had reported to Group Command that 504 Squadron were ready for action. Then the waiting began. In the flight hut – a crew hut with basic facilities: toilets, kettle, chairs, telephone – the pilots brewed tea and passed the nerve-wracking time as best they could. Some played poker or read the newspapers, while others gratefully went back to sleep, curled up on mattresses on the crew room floor.

As the sun climbed, the day promised to be warm and clear, beautiful late summer weather. Perfect for bombers! Yet, as the morning shuffled slowly by, the radar stations showed no sign of a German attack. Finally the squadron was told to stand down. Half relieved and half disappointed, the pilots were driven back to the Officers' Mess. Tired and scruffy from his early start, Arty headed for the bathroom. And there he was, in a steaming tub, wondering what on earth had happened to the war.

Scramble

Suddenly a loud rap on the door interrupted his thoughts.

'Quick, Ray, there's a flap on – we're on readiness again!'

(Readiness – ready to take off within five minutes.)

Cursing to himself, Arty leapt out of the bath. Without pausing to dry he squirmed into his uniform and ran for the truck, socks in hand. He was still struggling to pull them on when they screeched up to the flight hut.

It was 11:15 and the order to scramble had just come over the telephone from the Sector HQ at North Weald. As he announced this over the loudspeakers, the duty operator leaned over to the gramophone and put the squadron 'Scramble Song 'on the turntable. While Arty rushed to his locker and pulled on his life jacket and boots, the William Tell Overture blared out:

Diddle-um, diddle-um, diddle-um pom, pom.

Diddle-um, diddle-um, diddle-um pom, pom.

It was a 504 squadron joke: 'William Tell, run like hell.' The rousing music gave the pilots a buzz as they hurried to take off.

By the time Arty had sprinted to his Hurricane, the ground crew had started the roaring Merlin engine. In a blur of activity they helped him into the cockpit and parachute harness. His helmet was already plugged into the radio and oxygen supply as he rammed it over his bedraggled hair.

Waving chocks away, Arty taxied across the bumpy grass airstrip to the far end of the field. Hendon was a small station surrounded by houses and the Hurricanes needed every inch they could get to clear the rooftops. With the wind behind them and throttles rammed open the squadron soared into the air in an untidy gaggle. Had enemy fighters jumped them, they would have been helpless.

Once airborne, 504 formed up into A and B flights, two parallel lines of six planes. Arty was at the back in charge of Green section, B flight. They were the weavers, the rear guard, keeping look-out behind. Soon instructions came over the radio to climb to 17,000 feet and intercept a raid of 30 or more bombers closing in on London from the south-east.

Within minutes they were in sight, like a flock of sea-gulls in the distance. (German bombers flew in a V formation – a leader and two **wingmen**.) But they were coming up fast – Dornier 17s in a tight, disciplined formation. Arty quickly recognized their sinister shape – the large glass nose, looking angry and swollen compared to the slim fuselage and fragile-looking twin tail. 'Ugly beggars,' he thought.

'Tally Ho!'

Abruptly the radio crackled into life, 'Tally Ho!' The enemy had been sighted. As each Hurricane swooped in, the pilots picked their targets and opened fire. By the time Arty piled in from the back of the group the sky was already a crazy jumble of wheeling and jostling aircraft.

Although the German bombers were slow, they were far from helpless. Flying through a fierce barrage, Arty got a Dornier in the orange circle of his sights. He pushed hard on the gun button and his plane shook as the eight Browning machine-guns spat out a storm of bullets. Even a short burst was enough to rip through an enemy aircraft, and it was important not to waste bullets. Hurricanes only carried enough ammunition for 14 seconds firing time.

Air combat was fast and furious. A pilot who needed time to think, 'What do I do now?' would not last long. That was why so many rookie pilots were shot down on their first mission. But Arty was a survivor. Even as he pressed his gun button he was ready for the next problem — breaking off the attack safely. If he overshot the bomber he would expose the vulnerable belly of his Hurricane to the German gunners. Instead, the split second he stopped firing, he banked sharply left and dived steeply.

As his plane dropped, Arty checked to make sure no one was on his tail. Good, all clear. He breathed deeply to ease the fierce pressure crushing his chest and levelled out. Now it was time to climb back into the fight. But what fight? As he scanned the sky above it was empty. His dive had carried him out of sight of the dozens of raging planes . . . or had it? As he glanced west, he saw three Dorniers in a tight V formation. He guessed they were the original leaders of the German bomber group, still on course for London. And since there were no other British fighters in sight, he would have to stop them!

Arty opened the throttle and raced after the Dorniers, a plan already forming in his mind. Charge up from behind, guns blazing? No that would be suicide — a mad rush into the tracks of their rear guns. A flanking manoeuvre to take out the port wingman? Much better! Moving almost as fast as thought, Arty crabbed in at an angle, so that his target shielded him from the fire of the other bombers.

It worked. He opened fire at 400 yards and smoke soon engulfed the Hurricane. The bomber was hit. Wait! This wasn't smoke. It was oil. Thick black oil right across his canopy. He couldn't see a blinking thing. Blind! Instinctively he shut the throttle and prayed. Even so, in the moments it took for the air stream to blast the oil free Arty came close to disaster. When his vision cleared, a huge shape blotted out the sky. It was the Dornier, slowing down fast — and he was about to ram into it. Desperately Arty shoved the control lever forward, so fiercely that he felt the shoulder straps of his safety harness bite into his collarbone. With inches to spare the Hurricane ducked under the bomber, barely escaping the propellers.

As the stricken bomber glided slowly downwards, Arty turned his attention to the remaining pair. He would go for the other wingman first. Swinging over to the starboard side he roared forward and closed in for another attack. His first burst was bang on target and flames rippled down the Dornier. Suddenly there was a flicker of white! Someone trying to bale out? Then Arty lost control, the Hurricane was heaving about like a mad creature. Fighting the stick he levelled his plane and anxiously looked for damage. No. It couldn't be! Incredibly a German was hanging from his port wing, trapped by his parachute canopy.

Arty had never really thought about the enemy he hunted every day. They were invaders, but the battles were nothing personal. Just kill or be killed. Suddenly this poor devil was dangling from his wing at over 250 mph. He had to help him. He jerked the joystick from side to side, waggling the wings, but nothing happened. Something more violent was needed. Using hard right rudder he slewed the plane to starboard. Slowly at first, then in a flash, the parachute slid along the wing edge and dropped away.

There was no time to see if it opened cleanly, or if the German plummeted to his death – the third Dornier was still heading for central London. Arty was worried. Why hadn't the pilot turned to run for France? Only one bomber left out of more than 30. It was reckless to carry on alone. Was this Nazi on a suicide mission? Buckingham Palace had been hit a few days before, but no one had been hurt. Was he trying to finish off the Royal family? And if his bombs missed the Palace, what about the innocent civilians who might be killed?

Another splatter of oil smeared Arty's canopy. Only a little, but it set his heart pounding. This wasn't German oil. It was coming from the Hurricane. His plane had been hit too. As its lifeblood seeped away the Merlin engine began to run roughly, the rev counter surging. How long before it seized up? He had to act now before he was forced to land.

Ignoring the warning growls from the engine he opened the throttle and tore past the Dornier – only to turn and face it, almost but not quite, head on. A frontal attack was the best of all. It took nerves of steel, but gave him the chance to fire at point-blank range into the enemy cockpit. As the two planes closed in at over 500 mph Arty hit the gun button. The Brownings drummed ... and died. He was out of ammo.

A wave of dismay swept over Arty. In seconds he would have to break away to avoid a collision and the bomber would escape ... unless? ... Unless? The German tail-plane looked thin and weak. Almost before he had the idea Arty aimed his left wing at the nearest fin. The Hurricane was a tough kite, renowned for the punishment it could take. He would knock this Dornier for six, like a footballer tripping an opponent.

Crunch! Yet not much of a crunch. Amazing! He'd got away with it. The Hurricane dipped and he moved the control lever to correct it. Nothing! The nose fell. Arty jerked the control lever left and right. Again nothing. The plane was plunging straight down. Elation turned to shock. Far from getting away with it, the gallant aircraft was finished, all control gone.

Arty's Hurricane and a Dornier collide in mid-air.

Bale Out

In seconds the Hurricane had dropped almost 8,000 feet, tearing towards the ground at over 400 mph. Time to bail out! This was his first time for real, but Arty knew the drill. He unlocked and slid back the hood, undid the safety harness and heaved himself out of his seat. His head and body thrust into a thunderous vortex. The buffeting was so hard that at first he thought he had been sucked into the propeller. Yet something held him tight. He had forgotten to unplug the radio lead to his helmet.

With every instinct screaming, NO! NO! he struggled back into the cockpit and freed the lead. But fate had decided to play with Arty. As he fought his way out a second time, a blast jammed him backwards over the fuselage and snagged his parachute inside the cockpit. He knew that he was tearing towards the earth and kicked frantically against the control column. Suddenly the Hurricane began to spin and he was clear, thrown out by centrifugal force. He was clear, but clear did not mean safe.

As he shot out into the air, the tail of the plane clipped Arty's shoulder. He barely felt the blow, was only vaguely aware that his right arm and shoulder had gone numb; hardly realized he had been hurt – until he tried to pull the ripcord of his parachute. Arty's fingers closed over the D-ring, but he had no strength to tug it. Urgently he gripped his right wrist with his left hand and jerked. For what seemed an age nothing happened and then there was an explosion above him. The chute opened so hard that his boots flew off.

As Arty gazed upwards he could see the Dornier falling in lazy spirals, with the whole tail section sheared off. No wonder his plane had been damaged by the impact. Glancing down he could see the Hurricane about to slam into – my God! Central London. He was stunned to find he was only a few hundred feet over Victoria Station. His lone battle had been above thick cloud and he had not known that the last bomber had reached its target area.

With horror, Arty saw he was dropping straight towards a maze of electrified railway lines. Losing height rapidly, he pulled the rigging and veered towards a three-storey block of flats. If luck was on his side, he might just drift over them and land in the road ... THWACK! No luck. He hit the ridge tiles.

At first the chute billowed up, giving enough lift to support his weight. For a few shaky seconds he balanced on the slates, like a mad puppet. Then the chute collapsed and he slipped and rolled. With the edge looming, Arty scrabbled frantically for a hand-hold. After all he had been through it seemed he might break his neck falling off a roof.

With a last gasp, he grabbed at the guttering ... missed ... and toppled over. He hadn't time to scream before a wrenching jolt stopped his fall. Looking down he saw both legs were inside an empty dustbin. Looking up he saw his parachute wrapped around the top of the drainpipe. He was safe. His only injuries were his shoulder ... and his dignity.

A Home Guard Sergeant escorted Arty to see what was left of his Hurricane. It had come down at a crossroads and miraculously missed nearby buildings. The plane had plunged 5 m into the ground.

FIGHTING FACTS

Arty and the Flame Thrower

Years later Arty found out that on that late summer Sunday he had almost been the victim of a German secret weapon. Remember the oil that covered his canopy, blinding him? It wasn't from the damaged engine of a Dornier, the plane had been carrying an experimental flame thrower. The oil should have ignited and burned him to death.

What about the Germans?
The Dornier that Arty rammed was the first German aircraft brought down over central London. The crew survived – they bailed out, landing in the Oval cricket ground. The bomber crashed into Victoria Station.

Last Push by Luftwaffe
In the week after the first mass raid on London the Germans sensed victory.

Score Line
On 11 and 14 of September, Fighter Command and Luftwaffe losses were almost the same:

11 September – Score Line
Great Britain	29
Germany	25

14 September – Score Line
Great Britain	14
Germany	14

Better still, German pilots reported scrappy attacks by the RAF. Was this the collapse they had been expecting for weeks? Goering hoped that one more push would finish the job.

15 September

Morning Mayhem

Around 10:50 radar blips showed a big raid building up over the French coast. Amazingly the Germans spent half an hour sorting their formations out – 100 bombers, escorted by 400 Me 109 fighters. This gave ample time for the RAF to prepare a warm welcome.

The enemy planes were harried from the moment they crossed the coast, all the way to London. The climax of the battle came just before noon. Four squadrons of Hurricanes attacked the bombers (including Arty's 504 Squadron) while the famous pilot, Douglas Bader, who had lost his legs earlier in the war and flew with artificial limbs, led a 'Big Wing' of five squadrons of Spitfires against the Me 109s. This was a total of 60 planes. Many of the raiders simply dumped their bombs and turned for home.

Afternoon Anger

The British pilots had barely time to snatch a cup of tea and a bully beef sandwich before they were in the air again. A second attack came in at 14:00 – around 150 bombers and 300 fighters. This time, the Luftwaffe armada was hit by 170 RAF fighters over Kent. Above the hop fields, the sky became thick with the plumes of whirling dogfights as the 109s fought to protect the bombers.

Then, as the German planes neared the southern outskirts of London the battle became a rout. Just as the 109s were running out of fuel and turning for France, another twelve Squadrons of Hurricanes and Spitfires roared into sight. Stunned, most of the bomber pilots took the only sensible action to avoid a bloodbath – they dropped their bombs at random and ran.

15 September – Score Line

Fighter Command shot down 61
Luftwaffe shot down 29

Sea Lion Sunk

On the day when Luftwaffe pilots believed they had come to finish off the 'last fifty Spitfires', they found themselves facing over 300 fighters. It was clear that Fighter Command was far from beaten. Forty-eight hours later, Hitler postponed Operation Sea Lion, until 1941 at the earliest. Although enemy raids lasted until the end of October, 15 September is seen as the day the RAF won – 'Battle of Britain Day'.

Hurricane – The Forgotten Plane

The sleek Spitfire usually steals the glory in histories of the Battle of Britain. The Spitfire was the faster plane, but more than half the fighting was done by Hurricanes,

Fighter Command Aircraft during the Battle of Britain

Type	Max. Speed	Range	Weapons	Comment
Hawker Hurricane Mk I	324 mph (520 kph) at 15,650 ft	505 miles (815 km)	Eight .303 inch machine-guns in the wings.	Pilots liked the Hurricane because it could take a lot of punishment and still get them home.
Supermarine Spitfire Mk IA	365 mph (585 kph) at 19,000 ft (5,790 m)	575 miles (925 km)	Eight .303 inch machine-guns in the wings.	The perfect fighter combining grace, speed, flexibility and firepower.
Boulton Paul Defiant	304 mph at 17,000 ft (490 kph) 17,000 ft (5,180 m)	465 miles (750 km)	Four .303 inch machine-guns in a turret behind the cockpit.	Only two squadrons were equipped with Defiants during the battle and they took heavy losses.
Bristol Blenheim, twin-engined fighter	278 mph (475 kph) at 15,000 ft (4,570 m)	1,050 miles (1,690 km)	Five machine-guns firing forward and one in the rear turret.	Six squadrons of Blenheim light bombers were converted to fighters.

designed by Sydney Camm at Hawker Engineering. The prototype made its first flight in 1935, reaching a speed of 315 mph (505 kph) at 16,000 feet (4,875 m). By September 1939 the RAF had 500 Hurricanes in service. Like the Spitfire, the heart of the Hurricane was the powerful Rolls Royce Merlin engine. In July 1940, three out of five of the 700 RAF fighters were Hurricanes.

Bad Landings

Many pilots during the Battle of Britain faced their worst nightmare – being shot down. For some this meant death or capture – while others had amazing escapes and were back in action within a few days.

Trapped!

On 9 July, New Zealander Flight Lieutenant Al Deere had a narrow escape. During a dogfight over the Channel he collided with an Me 109. Astonishingly both planes survived but Al's Spitfire was badly damaged. He remembered, 'the force of the impact pitched me violently forward on to my cockpit harness, the straps of which bit viciously into my shoulders. At the same moment, the control column was snatched abruptly from my gripping fingers.' As smoke poured into the cockpit Al tried to bale out, only to find that the hood would not release. Trapped, he had no choice but to try an emergency landing – before he burned to death. Trailing clouds of smoke and flame he headed for the coast and crashed into a cornfield. Fear then gave him almost superhuman strength. With his bare hands, he smashed a hole in the Perspex canopy and clawed his way out.

Al led a charmed life. On 15 August he was shot down and baled out over Deal. Two weeks later, on 31 August, he was taking off from Hornchurch when a bomb burst near his Spitfire and blew it over. He wrote:

*To this day I am not exactly clear what happened next.
What I do remember is the impact with the ground
and a terrifying period of ploughing along the ground
upside down.*

Bandaged and battered, Al was back in action the next day.

Shooting Pilots

On 15 August, Australian Hurricane pilot Johnny Cock of 87 Squadron, was hit over the sea near Portsmouth. Fellow pilot Denis David watched angrily as an Me 109 tried to kill him in mid-air as he baled out. Denis remembered:

*His parachute cords went ping! ping! ping! – beginning
to separate him from his chute canopy – as the bullets
flew around him. I managed to get behind the murder-
ous Hun and shoot him down. I circled Johnny till he hit
the water ...*

The bodies of several RAF pilots who baled out were recovered riddled with bullets. One case was 'Wilkie' Wilkinson of 266 Squadron. He collided with a 109 on 18 August and, according to witnesses, he baled out and seemed unhurt. Yet when his body was found it was full of bullet holes. In spite of this, British airmen did not fire at enemy pilots who were parachuting to safety. However, the RAF slate was not completely clean.

Fighter Command pilots were under orders to shoot down German rescue seaplanes — even if they were plucking Luftwaffe aircrew from the Channel. Worse, Polish and Czech pilots, who deeply hated the Germans, could not be stopped from taking pot shots whenever they had the chance.

German and British Pilots' Jargon

Luftwaffe Language
Bleat – open fire with a machine gun
Cannon – an ace pilot
Crew – flying family
Dismount hot – to be shot down in flames
Eggs – bombs
Emil – Messerschmitt 109E fighter
Glow worms – searchlights
Indians – enemy aircraft
Measles – anti-aircraft fire
Rabbit – stupid officer
Tommies – British

RAF Jargon
Angels – height at which to fly in thousands of feet
Bandits – enemy aircraft identified
Bogey – unidentified aircraft
Crumpet – girl
Dogfight – air battle
Jerries – Germans
Readiness – combat ready to take off within five minutes
Scramble – take off at once
Shiners – barrage balloons
Tally ho – target sighted
Vector – turn on to specified course

BOMBERS OVER BERLIN

BATTLE BRIEFING

Bomber Command

Even before the Battle of Britain was over Winston Churchill wanted to hit back against Nazi-dominated Europe. But how was this to be done? The British had no allies left on the continent, and their army was no match for German troops. This left only one way of taking the fighting to the enemy — bombers.

In the early months of the war RAF Bomber Command was equipped with slow, twin-engined planes — Whitleys, Wellingtons and Hampdens. They could only deliver small bomb loads and suffered heavy losses to German fighters during daylight raids. Switching to night attacks cut casualties but brought other problems. Photographs showed that most bombs missed and were doing little damage to the factories and transport systems that were the main targets.

It was not until 1942 that Bomber Command became a real threat. A tough new Commanding Officer, Air Marshall Arthur 'Bomber' Harris took over to carry out a ruthless war aim. His orders from the government were blunt:

The primary objective of your operations is to break the **morale** of the civilian population, and in particular of the industrial workers ... the aiming points are to be the built-up areas, not for instance, the dockyards or aircraft factories.

In reality this meant: bomb German cities into the ground. In British eyes this was only equal to the savage Luftwaffe raids on London, Liverpool, Coventry and dozens of other towns. The Germans would reap what they had sown.

A range of new weapons and inventions were coming on stream to do the job. The mighty, four-engined Avro Lancaster could carry loads of up to 14,000 lb (6,350 kg) over a range of 1,040 miles (1,673 km). And Harris was promised a fleet of 4,000 bombers to reduce Germany to rubble. Hitting targets remained a problem but a series of devices helped. The 'Gee' radio navigation system guided raids to the target area while the H2S airborne radar set gave a map-like picture of the ground below.

In May 1942 1,047 bombers devastated Cologne. In 90 minutes 2,500 fires burnt out 3,330 buildings, killing 469 people and making 45,000 more homeless. Soon many

An Avro Lancaster.

other German cities were burning too – Dusseldorf, Essen, Frankfurt, Hamburg, Lubeck, Rostock.

In 1943–44, as Bomber Command grew in strength and confidence, the main target became the German capital – Berlin! The name was enough to make experienced bomber crews wince. A mission to 'The Big City' meant big trouble. Berlin was deep inside Germany, so deep that raiders could only be sure of getting there and back in the dark on long winter nights. It was heavily defended too – anti-aircraft guns and searchlights ringed the city, while night fighters prowled the black skies. The brave airmen went into action knowing that many of them would not be coming home again.

TARGET BERLIN

The evening of 15 February 1944 was cold and overcast. In this cheerless gloom, 891 heavily loaded Lancaster and Halifax bombers prepared for take-off. RAF Bomber Command had been fighting the 'Battle of Berlin' since November 1943. This was the fifteenth raid of the winter and would be the heaviest. It was one more step in the relentless plan to pound the German capital to ruins – the RAF attacking by night and the American air force, the USAF, by day.

Slowly, like lumbering ducks, the bombers reached take-off speed – 110 mph (175 kph) and clawed their way into the air. The throb of Merlin engines echoed for miles around dozens of aerodromes dotted across the eastern side of England. It took well over an hour for all

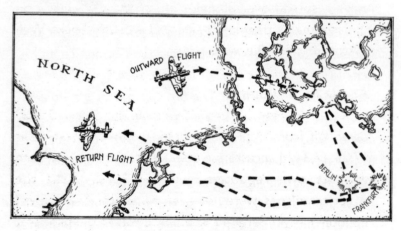

The routes to and from Berlin.

the planes to get airborne and even longer for them to climb into formation. In thousands of nearby homes families glanced at one another as they huddled close to their cosy fires. They knew what the distant roar meant. The cheerful Air Force 'lads' they met in the local shop or pub were going to war. Many comforted themselves with the thought, 'Jerry's going to get a pasting.' Yet what would be the cost? Which faces would be missing the following day?

That night's route took the Main Force out over the North Sea, across southern Denmark and the Baltic before swinging abruptly south to Berlin. It meant a gruelling eight-hour return flight. Another 24 Lancasters headed for Frankfurt-on-Oder, a diversion to draw off some of the German night fighters. But the enemy was not to be fooled. At 18:16 the first British bombers were picked up by German radar. Soon the whole bomber stream, spread over 80 miles of sky, showed clearly on the screens. With ample warning, the deadly Focke-Wulf 190s and Junker 88s were waiting.

Aussie Air Gunner

Lancaster ND444 GT-O of 156 Pathfinder Squadron had taken off from Warboys airfield in Cambridgeshire at 17:26. (7,377 Lancasters were built during the war, each with its own registration number. Most, unlike the American planes, were not given names by their crews.) Londoner Flight Sergeant Ken Doyle was in the pilot seat and Australian Flight Sergeant Geoffrey C. C. Smith was rear gunner. Geoff had been in the artillery until 1942 when he joined the RAAF (Royal Australian Air Force). The following year he was posted to Britain, just in time for the assault on Berlin. Ken was glad that the Aussie was 'Tail-End Charlie', the main defence of the 'Lanc'. Geoff was one of the best – cool, calm and alert. He had survived over 20 missions and already had one night fighter to his credit, a Junkers 88 shot down on 2 December.

Pilot – Flight Sergeant Ken Doyle
Rear gunner – Flight Sergeant Geoffrey C. C. Smith
Upper turret gunner – Sergeant Nobby Clarke
Wireless operator – Sergeant Don Green
Navigator – Sergeant Winlow
Flight engineer – Sergeant Syd Richardson
Bomb aimer – Sergeant Alf Astle

The crew of Lancaster ND444 GT-O in order of appearance in this chapter.

Ken was right, experience counted. Thirty miles from Berlin Geoff snapped out a warning over the intercom, 'Fighter coming in.' He had spotted an Me 110 dead astern and 650 m below. Yet spotted was hardly the word. The fighter's red and green navigation lights flicked on and off. The German might as well have carried a neon sign flashing 'Here I am'. It was too easy. He was either a fool, suicidal or ...

'There's two of them,' Geoff yelled. 'I'll watch this one. Look out for the other Jerry, Nobby.'

Nobby Clarke was upper turret gunner. He had

Tail-End Charlie on a 'Lanc' in his Fraser-Nash rear gun turret.

barely time to scan the darkness before all hell let loose.

'Skipper. Corkscrew Port! Go! Go! Go!' the Australian commanded. The 110 had suddenly closed in – firing! Ken obeyed at once. In an attack from behind the rear gunner gave the orders. (Corkscrewing was a violent emergency manoeuvre to lose attacking fighters. The plane flipped sharply to one side and dived almost vertically before levelling out again.) As the Lancaster banked Geoff opened up. His four machine-guns tore into the fighter and abruptly it blew apart, the explosion illuminating the sky. But at almost the same moment glowing strings of green tracer whipped past Geoff's turret and he felt a stunning wave of pain surging from his right ankle. The other Jerry had made his move.

Geoff's order to corkscrew hadn't come a second too soon. A Focke-Wulf had pounced, pumping a hail of cannon shells along the length of the Lancaster's fuselage. As the second fighter disappeared into the night the RAF bomber was left stricken. The hydraulic lines were cut and the escaping hydraulic oil burst into flames. Left without power both turrets and the bomb doors were almost useless. Nobby's left leg was broken by a cannon shell and riddled with steel splinters. As he fell the oxygen line was ripped from his face-mask and he passed out. Geoff was writhing in agony – he had been hit by a cannon shell that had almost severed his foot.

Heading Home

The fighter attack and the bomber's escape were over in seconds, but they were seconds that changed the mission. As soon as Ken levelled out he began to assess the damage. Anxiously he called each crewman on the intercom. There was no reply from Nobby, and he could hear Geoff groaning in the rear turret. The first decision was the hardest. With the bomb doors jammed it was clear that pushing on to Berlin was pointless. Only 15 miles from the target Ken turned reluctantly for England. Now it was time to patch up the crew and the almost defenceless aircraft.

The wireless operator, Sergeant Don Green, went back to help Nobby, who was gasping for air. Don slipped a spare oxygen lead into the gunner's mouth, made him comfortable and took his place. The navigator, Sergeant Winlow, went to investigate the fire and rescue Geoff. With relief, he found the only thing still burning was the Australian's parachute. Using an extinguisher he put out the blaze and then tried to persuade Geoff to leave his precious guns. Incredibly, although he was losing a lot of blood, the stubborn Aussie refused. Geoff knew there was still a high risk of another fighter attack. In spite of the pain and the lack of power he could still operate his turret by hand. While they were over enemy territory he insisted he was going to stay put.

Luckily the crew of ND444 avoided the further unwelcome attentions of the Luftwaffe but their troubles were far from over. As they neared the coast they came under intense fire from anti-aircraft guns. Flak burst around the Lanc and two engines were hit. Ken promptly shut them down, but now they were limping home. If either of the surviving Merlins played up they would be ditching in the freezing North Sea.

The next snag was to dump the bombs. The last thing they wanted was an emergency landing with a full bomb load. A crash or a fire and . . . BOOM! Sergeant Syd Richardson, the flight engineer, crawled into the bomb bay inspection hatch and dismantled the connections to the wrecked hydraulic system. In theory, when they jettisoned the bombs, their weight should force open the bomb doors. The theory worked – almost. The deadly load fell away cleanly into the sea, except for one jammed 500 lb (220 kg) bomb. Syd had done wonders but the landing had better be smooth.

Once over the coast it was also time to prise Geoff out of his turret. And it wasn't going to be easy. The flip doors into the gun turret had frozen solid and the only thing to do was chop through them with a fire axe. For over half an hour bomb aimer Sergeant Alf Astle, helped by Don Green, hacked at the doors until they had made a gap big enough to drag Geoff through. They were horrified when they peered inside. His smashed leg was entangled in the ammunition belts and the turret seemed to have been sprayed with blood. When they pulled him out they gave Geoff a shot of **morphine** to ease the pain and he slipped into a merciful sleep. Now all they needed was a safe landing, but the odds did not look good.

Ken radioed ahead for permission to land at the emergency runway at Woodbridge on the Suffolk coast. As they approached his thoughts raced through the problems facing him. The undercarriage had been shot up. Although it had lowered, would it collapse when he touched down? Then there were the bomb doors. Still open, they dragged like an enormous brake. The trim of the plane had gone to pot. And best not to even think about the bomb still aboard.

Grimly, Ken alerted the airfield that they better give

him plenty of room for a belly landing. Finally he warned the crew they were going in and asked them to do what they could to protect the injured gunners. Tenderly, they packed themselves around Nobby and Geoff and braced for impact.

At 1:50 the Lancaster touched down, the engines revving hard to avoid stalling. The starboard tyre burst and the plane slewed a little but the undercarriage held. To Ken's amazement they were down in one piece.

At once the crew sprang into action. They chopped a large hole in the fuselage and lifted the wounded men into a waiting ambulance. Geoff was rushed to Ely hospital but his leg was too badly damaged to save – it was amputated above the knee. The stubborn gunner was awarded a CGM (Conspicuous Gallantry Medal) for staying at his post to protect his Lancaster and crew. As usual his reaction was modest. 'If it hadn't been for the skipper, we'd never have got back at all.'

In 1945 Geoff Smith returned to Australia and became a successful businessman. He didn't let his lack of a leg get him down, always believing, 'I'm as good as the next guy.' But sadly this story doesn't have a happy ending for everyone. In war, fate is never fair and one brush with danger doesn't guarantee safety in the future. Ken Doyle, Alf Astle and Don Green were killed in September 1944 on a mission over Calais. Their plane was hit by flak and crashed in the sea. Their bodies were never found.

FIGHTING FACTS

The Cost

Of the 891 bombers that took off on Geoff Smith's raid, 42 were shot down and two crashed in England. That was almost 5 per cent of the total force – light losses. During the next raid on Berlin, on 21 March, 72 planes were lost out of 809, almost 9 per cent. Throughout the war 56,000 aircrew of RAF Bomber Command were killed. Of these, 40 per cent came from the Commonwealth and other countries that rallied to the Allied cause.

Turret Terrors

The rear turret of the bomber was the most dangerous place on the plane. Most Luftwaffe pilots preferred to attack from behind and slightly below. If they killed the rear gunner in their first burst the bomber was helpless. Worse, the German night fighters had better weapons. Their 20 mm or 30 mm cannon had more firing power and a longer range than the dated British machine-guns.

Top Tips for Rear Turret Gunners

Gunners learned by experience and passed tips on to one another. Good advice from old hands saved the lives of new recruits:

- Remember the rear turret is the coldest place on the plane, sometimes down to – 40 degrees at 15,000 feet (4,500 m). Watch out for frostbite. Wear as much clothing as possible – silk underwear, woollen pullovers, extra woollen socks, electrically heated suit. You'll feel like the **Michelin Man** but every layer is vital.

- Cover all your exposed flesh in lanolin and wear elastoplast on your cheeks to stop the metal studs on your flying helmet from freezing to your skin.
- Wear sunglasses for half an hour before take-off to get your eyes used to night vision.
- Always carry a 'panic bowler', a steel helmet – not for your head, stupid! Put it in your seat cushion to protect your most important bits.
- Make sure the perspex canopy is spotlessly clean. Watch out for old perspex, it scratches easily and can be difficult to see through. Best take out the rear-centre panel. OK, it's a lot colder, if that seems possible, but you get a clear view. It's your choice, freeze or die.
- Shave before take-off. Stubble can be irritating inside a rubber face oxygen mask. And don't forget to squeeze the oxygen tube regularly during the flight. If ice crystals form and block the tube you might pass out. If no one revives you quickly, that's it, mate.
- Remember good luck charms and rituals before take-off – a little of your girlfriend's perfume, a love letter, a rabbit's foot, a Cornish pixie, a silver three-penny bit. Yeah, it's stupid, but you never know . . .
- If a night fighter attacks – wait, wait, WAIT! His cannon have a longer range, but he needs to get close to

be sure of a kill. Let him come in to 500 yards or less if you've got the nerve. Then let him have it.

Main Bomber Command aircraft in the Battle of Britain

Type	Max. Speed	Range	Weapons	Comment
Avro Lancaster	281 mph (450 kph) at 11,000 ft (3,353 m) with extra fuel and 7,000 lb (3,175 kg) bomb load	1,040 miles (1,670 km) or 2,680 miles (4,310 km)	14,000 lb (6,350 kg) bomb load. Eight .303 machine-guns.	A large stable plane that could take a lot of punishment. The backbone of Bomber Command from 1943.
Mosquito	408 mph (655 kph) at 26,000 ft (9,048 m)	1,370 miles (2,200 km)	4,000 lb (1,800 kg)	A fast, light bomber, built from plywood. No guns were fitted in the bomber version, because it could out-run most fighters.
Handley-Page Halifax Mk I	265 mph (426 kph)	1,860 miles (2990 km) at 17,500 ft (5,334m) with 5,800 lb bomb load	5,800 lb (2,635 kg) bomb load. Eight .303 machine-guns.	The first true heavy bomber produced in large numbers for the RAF.

One City Too Far

The plan to bomb Germany into submission was controversial during World War II and has been argued about ever since. But the destruction of one city above all others has come to symbolize the cruelty of war – Dresden.

Dresden was the capital of Saxony, in southern Germany. It was an ancient town with many wooden buildings and a maze of narrow streets in the centre. By early 1945 it was packed with refugees and troops running away from Russian armies. Although it had no major industries, Bomber Command was running out of new targets and Dresden came up on the hit list. On the night of 13/14 February 805 aircraft attacking in two waves dropped 2,659 tons of high explosive and incendiary (fire) bombs. During daylight on 14 and 15 February the Americans blitzed the city again with 600 more bombers. The results were horrendous. A fire-storm swept Dresden and 35,000 people died.

Repairing the Scars of War

One British bomber pilot, 31-year-old Flight Lieutenant Frank Smith of 57 Squadron, looked down from his plane at the blazing city and shuddered. He was haunted by his part in the raids on Dresden for the rest of his life. His son Alan remembers: 'In his eyes it was nothing to boast about. He tried to instil in us all as children the horror of it all.'

Frank died in 1982, but eighteen years later in a strange twist of fate, Alan Smith found himself helping to repair the scars of war. On 14 February 2000, the 55th anniversary of the raids, he presented Dresden with an 8m-high golden cross and orb. This will sit atop the city's most famous church, the Frauenkirche. This medieval

The ruins of Dresden.

masterpiece was destroyed in 1945 and is still being rebuilt. The massive project will last until 2006.

Alan worked for a London firm of silversmiths and was delighted when they won the contract to make the new cross. This cost £300,000, and in an act of reconciliation the money was raised in Britain. When the 1.25-ton cross was finished, his boss couldn't think of anyone more fitting than a bomber pilot's son to present it. After the solemn handover Alan commented, 'My father would have been filled with pride. My family and I want to say sorry for what happened.'

THE YANKS ARE COMING

BATTLE BRIEFING

Eighth Air Force

In December 1941 the United States was dragged into World War II by the shock Japanese attack on Pearl Harbor. In spite of this, the Americans agreed that the greatest danger came from Germany and that Hitler should be defeated first. Like the British, they believed that the war could be won by the relentless use of bombers.

In February 1942 Major-General Carl Spaatz arrived in Britain to set up the European wing of the United States Army Air Force – the Eighth Air Force. Within a year over 100 new airfields had been built across East Anglia and 'round the clock bombing' of Germany was under way – the Americans by day and the British by night. 'Snuffy' Smith was one of the army of American 'flyboys' posted to England in 1943.

'SNUFFY' SMITH

Ball Turret Gunner

No one could remember how Sergeant 'Snuffy' Smith got his nickname. In fact, before 1 May 1943 there wasn't anything much to remember about Snuffy at all. His real name was Maynard Harrison Smith. He was small, slim and neat – a tax clerk from Carol, Michigan, where he lived with his parents on South State Street.

Snuffy enlisted in the United States Army Air Force in 1942 and trained as a crewman for bombers. His size meant he was selected as a gunner for the ball turret of a Boeing B-17 Fortress – a cramped, perspex and metal globe hung under the fuselage of the plane. He was 32, an 'old man' amongst thousands of 18 and 19-year-old recruits. Perhaps a little too old, because he didn't suffer Air Force discipline easily and earned a reputation as an awkward character.

In the spring of 1943 Snuffy was sent to England and assigned to the 423rd Bombardment Squadron – a unit of the 'Mighty' Eighth Air Force in England. The British bombed Germany under protection of darkness but the Americans were convinced they could hit the enemy harder with daylight raids. So from August 1942 ever-larger formations of heavily armed bombers probed into France and then Germany itself. The cost was high.

B-17 bombers carried a crew of ten and bristled

A B-17 in flight.

with machine-guns. To give mutual protection they flew in tight box formations of eighteen aircraft and could lay down awesome firepower if jumped from astern or abeam. Yet they were easy meat for Nazi fighters, especially the fearsome Focke-Wulf Fw 190s. German pilots soon learned that a head on attack – a sharp burst of cannon shells into the cockpit – meant a quick end to a bomber. Snuffy and the other new recruits were all too often filling the gaps caused by mounting losses.

First Mission

On 1 May the 423rd Bombardment Squadron was ordered to join 60 other B-17s in an attack on the French port of St Nazaire, a base for U-boats – German submarines. 1st Lieutenant Lewis Page Johnson, skipper of Fortress 42-29649, hoped for an easy ride. It was his last combat flight before his tour of duty, 25 missions, was complete. The USA beckoned.

Many American bombers were boldly decorated – with names like Pistol Packin' Mama or Yankee Doodle. Johnson would have none of this. He didn't want anything on his plane that might make a Jerry fighter look twice. It was to this careful pilot that Snuffy was assigned for his first mission.

The raid ran like clockwork. No fighters and only light

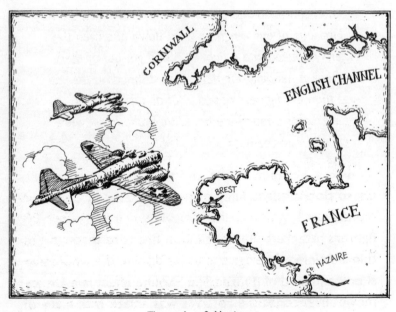

The attack on St Nazaire.

flak (anti-aircraft fire). The gleaming bombers reached their target, released their bombs and turned for home. They were over water and could see land ahead. Surely this meant England and safety! Johnson even joked that they'd have to ditch in the sea so he'd have a good story to tell his kids. In the history of mistimed wit, this quip was a whammy. Suddenly, all hell let loose.

Unknowingly, the B-17s had left St Nazaire in the wrong direction and flown towards the Brest Peninsula. They were still over France! As the Fortress crossed the coastline a hail of flak burst around the formation. Co-pilot Bob McCallum recalled:

> We had stumbled into a French port – navigator's error ... First one of our wingmen went down and then the other. We pulled into a tight turn and got out of there. We took a heading due north and stepped on the gas. And then the fighters ripped in at about 3 o'clock (above right) through the haze. We broke away, went right down on the deck and hedge hopped to shake the Jerries off. It worked.

Or so Bob thought. They turned north for England and he had just begun to breathe again when more Fw 190 fighters attacked. 20 mm cannon fire tore through the thin aluminium fuselage and to his dismay 'the whole ship shook and kind of bonged, like a sound effect in a Disney movie'. In seconds the Fortress was ablaze with many of the controls shot out. Captain Ray J. Check, flying another plane close by, later reported: 'Except for the nose and cockpit, flames completely filled the ship . . . it was like a comet.'

The first Snuffy knew of the threat was enemy tracer shells whipping past his turret. Moments later he was shaken by a huge explosion. Urgently, he tried the intercom to the Skipper – nothing. Next he tried to rotate the turret to climb out – nothing. The power was down. Slowly he hand-cranked himself into the fuselage and climbed out to see two fires raging, a fierce one in the radio compartment and a second smaller blaze in the tail section.

As the stunned gunner tried to take in what was happening, the radio operator staggered out of his tiny compartment and dived out of the gun hatch. Snuffy knew he was jumping to almost certain death: 'Even though his chute opened, the poor guy's Mae West (life jacket) had been burned off and we were over plenty of water.'

Yet the horror of burning to death was so great that the port waist gunner had also tried to bale out but hadn't quite made it. He was trapped, half in and half out of the Fortress – his parachute harness snagged on his gun mounting.

'Hey, buddy, is it too hot for you?' Snuffy quipped as he pulled him back aboard.

The waist gunner stared at him as if he was mad and snapped, 'I'm getting out of here.'

There was no point in arguing. Snuffy helped him open

the rear escape hatch and watched as he jumped clear. He wished the crewman luck but had no time to waste, the smoke and gas in the plane were building up fast.

Firefighter

Despite the damage, the Fortress was flying level and Snuffy guessed the skipper must still be at the controls. With that hope in his mind, he decided to stay and fight the fires. Wrapping a sweater round his face to shield his eyes and throat, he grabbed an extinguisher and began to tackle the blaze in the radio compartment. At first the flames flared up but then slowly began to die away. Snuffy was just making headway when he glanced round to check the tail section – and saw movement. He recalled:

> I found the tail gunner painfully crawling back from his turret. I saw he had been hit in the back. I guessed a shell had gone through his left lung, so I laid him down on his left side to keep the blood from draining into his right lung and slowly drowning him. I gave him a shot of morphine and made him as comfortable as possible.

No sooner had Snuffy picked up the extinguisher again than another, more deadly, interruption appeared. He saw an Fw 190 zooming in from the side. With amazing cool, he gave it a burst from the right-waist gun and stepped across the plane to fire a second blast from the left-waist gun as the fighter swept underneath.

The next frantic minutes saw Snuffy leaping between tasks – fireman, gunner and paramedic. Using the remaining extinguishers he dowsed the forward blaze, spraying the last bottle over the smouldering control cables. The fuselage around the radio compartment was so badly damaged that large holes had been burned through the skin of the Fortress. Using these to his advantage he hurled smouldering wreckage and red-hot ammunition cans overboard.

Persistently, an Fw 190 pumped cannon shells into the stricken Fortress. Whether it was the same fighter, or newcomers joining in the kill, Snuffy couldn't tell. Each time he broke off and grabbed the nearest gun to return fire. Nervously he kept a couple of the hot ammunition cans to hand, ready to fend off any more visits by the Focke-Wulfs, but fearful in case they blew up.

Now Snuffy made a fateful decision. To move faster he took his parachute off and tied his fate to that of the plane and his wounded companion. With the Fortress flying at low altitude he wouldn't have time to put it on again before they crashed. Still, it was as well he hadn't removed it earlier. As he eased the pack off his aching back he saw it had stopped a bullet, probably from an exploding ammo can.

Turning to the smaller fire in the tail Snuffy faced a dangerous problem. The extinguishers were empty. Scrambling through the debris he found a water bottle and emptied it over the hottest part. After this there was nothing else to do but to try to smother the blaze with his hands and feet. Padding and stamping like a wild dancer he slowly snuffed it out – but not before his clothes had begun to smoulder.

Rough Landing

With the fire finally out Snuffy looked through a hatchway and caught his breath. He could see a coastline ahead and prayed that it was England. He knelt down and told the wounded tail gunner that safety was near but his own thoughts were not so confident. If they managed to locate an airfield would the battered plane survive a rough landing? Snuffy remembers:

I could tell she was acting tail heavy so I tossed overboard everything I could break loose – guns, ammunition, clothes, everything. I knew the tail wheel was gone and I was afraid the shock of the landing would break the 'Fort' in half.

In the cockpit Johnson had the same doubts. Bailing out seemed a good idea but he had two wounded crewmen in the nose section. Another option was ditching in the sea, but he was fairly sure the fire would have destroyed the dinghies. Like Snuffy he concluded he was there for the full ride.

After such a grim flight, any crew deserved a little good luck and Johnson sighed with relief when he saw an airfield ahead. It was Predannack in Cornwall. At least the navigation was correct this time. Now for the landing. Sweating with tension he brought the shattered Fortress in as easily as he could with the few remaining controls. With an ominous rumble she hit the runway – but held together. They were down.

When the wounded had been rushed to hospital, Johnson and Snuffy surveyed the damage:

- radio compartment and tail section burnt out;
- mid fuselage torn apart by cannon shells and internal fire;
- oxygen system ruptured – adding to the intensity of the fire;
- top turret disabled by cannon fire;
- tail wheel gear damaged;
- nose section shattered by cannon fire;
- petrol tank in port wing burnt out;
- No. 4 engine **nacelle** shot off.

It was quite a list. Johnson wouldn't have to make up any stories for his kids after all.

Difficult Hero
In his mission report Johnson gave fulsome praise to his turret gunner. He wrote: '... his acts performed in complete self-sacrifice were solely responsible for the safe return of the aeroplane, the life of the tail gunner and the lives of everyone else aboard.' As a result Snuffy was

awarded the Congressional Medal of Honour, only the second Eighth Air Force serviceman to win this rare honour.

Snuffy flew four more combat missions but he remained 'difficult to handle'. Only four days before the award ceremony, he was on punishment duty in the station mess hall. Imagine the embarrassment for the USAAF! The press loved the Snuffy story and he had become an all-American hero. But senior officers in the 423rd were almost relieved when he was withdrawn from service and sent home. Ironically, he was now far more useful touring the USA to rally the fighting spirit of the American public.

Old heroes are often forgotten, but not Snuffy. When he died in 1984 he was buried in Arlington National Cemetery with full military honours.

FIGHTING FACTS

Daylight Bombing

Heavy losses had convinced the RAF that night bombing was the only way to reduce casualties. In 1942, however, the Eighth Air Force arrived in Britain sure they had the planes and technology to bomb in daylight. These included:

- The Boeing B-17 heavy bomber, bristling with machine-guns and flying in box formations to give mutual covering fire.

- Self-regulating oxygen systems for the crew, and a turbo-supercharger for the engines, so that planes could fly at high altitudes – 25,000 feet and more.
- The Norden bombsight – an electro-mechanical computer that could 'drop a bomb into a pickle-barrel from 20,000 ft (6,095 m)'.

American Planes in the Daylight Battle Over Europe

Type	Max. Speed	Range	Weapons	Comment
Boeing B-17F Flying Fortress	299 mph (480 kph)	17,000 miles (27,350 km) at 30,000 ft (9,140 m) with Tokyo tanks (extra fuel tanks in the wings)	Up to thirteen .50 inch Browning machine-guns.	The 'Fort' could take heavy damage and was liked by crews.
North American P-51 Mustang	437 mph (705 kph) at 25,000 ft (7,620 m)	2,080 miles (3,345 km) with drop tanks	Six .05 calibre machine-guns.	The best Allied escort fighter of World War II.

Daylight Disappointment

The Eighth Air Force was in for a shock. German defences were far better than expected and the technology did not always work.

German fighters were armed with 20 mm or 30 mm cannon that could rip the aluminium structure of the B-17s apart.

Heavy 105 mm flak guns could hurl time-fused shells to a height of 31,000 feet (9,445 m), high enough to hit any Allied bomber.

The Norden bombsight had worked well on tests in sunny California, but in cloudy, rain-soaked European skies it was disappointing.

One in Three
In 1943–44 American losses were high. Two of the worst raids were on the small industrial town of Schweinfurt to knock out ball-bearing factories:

14 August 1943
Number of planes on mission	320
Number of planes shot down	60

17 August 1943
Number of planes on mission	230
Number of planes shot down	36

The Germans only lost 25 fighters.

A standard tour of duty for members of a bomber crew was 25 missions. That earned a ticket home! But with odds like those in the table, it was no wonder that aircrew believed they only had a one in three chance of surviving the tour.

Little Friends
It was soon clear that the bombers could not be expected to protect themselves against Nazi fighters. Escorts were needed. P-47 Thunderbolts and P-38 Lightnings were used at first but they barely had the

range to reach the German border. In December 1943 however, the answer roared in – the P-51 Mustang. Fitted with the Rolls Royce Merlin engine and drop tanks it became a war winner. By early 1944 the bomber crews, guarded by what they called their 'Little Friends', stood a far better chance of survival.

Combat Witness

I can say with truth I'd rather face a fighter than flak. A fighter you can do something about, but flak you can't.
John Butler of the 93rd Bombardment Group

The bombers had to stay on course – and once they were on their bomb-run, which was where the German fighters hit them, they couldn't deviate at all. They just had to plough on and when they were hit, they just blew right up, their whole bomb load went right up, and where an aeroplane had been there was just a smoke ring.
Lt-Colonel Jim Goodson of the 4th Fighter Group

His gun was frozen and he sat helplessly watching repeated fighter attacks ... the No.2 engine was hit and caught fire ... a plane on his wing went out of control ... and crashed into a bomber on their opposite side. The pilot had to take evasive action to miss pieces

*of B-17 that were flying in the air. He saw the ball
turret knocked off and go down like an apple with the
gunner still inside. He saw another man jump with a
burning parachute and go down like a lump of lead.*
Medical report on an exhausted gunner after a raid
on Kiel, 13 June 1943

Nose Art

Unlike Lieutenant Johnson, most American captains liked
a lively name and a vivid image painted on the nose of
their bombers. Some were given daring names:
KNOCK-OUT DROPPER
DEE-FEATER
HELLSADROPPIN
BOMB BOOGIE
Others were called after cartoon characters:
SNOW WHITE
MICKEY MOUSE
BUGS BUNNY
POPEYE
But pin-up girls were by far the most popular. The ruder
the better:
DINAH MIGHT
ICE COLD KATE
IZA VAILABLE
SLICK CHICK
HUSSLIN' HUSSY

East Anglia – USA

England was invaded during World War II – by friendly 'Yanks'. By June 1944 there were 300,000 Eighth Air Force personnel alone, most of them in East Anglia. Dozens of new airfields had to be built, each like a small town. A typical base needed a concrete runway a mile in length, two smaller back-up runways, hardstanding for the planes, 30 miles of drains, 500 separate buildings and a sewerage plant for 2,500 people. Most of these airfields were built by Irish navies or black GIs. (GI = General Infantryman or ordinary soldier.)

Memories of Britain

Rain

Most Americans hated the rain and dismal overcast skies. The 384th Bomb Group, based at Grafton Underwood in Northamptonshire, soon renamed their airfield Grafton Undermud.

Stinky Brits

A common view was that British bathrooms were primitive and underused. Some Yanks called England 'Goatland'.

Love

But the smell can't have been that bad. Love bloomed during the war. Around 35,000 British women married Americans and returned to the USA with them.

American servicemen were issued with guides on how to behave in Britain. Advice included:

- 'stop and think before you sound off about the lukewarm beer'
- 'don't show off or brag or bluster'
- 'don't make wisecracks about British defeats'
- 'don't make fun of British speech' and, most important of all,
- 'NEVER criticize the King or Queen.'

Rationing Riches

By 1943 rationing was biting hard in Britain, especially for children. Ice cream manufacture was banned from September 1942 until March 1945 and sweets were in short supply. In contrast the Americans seemed like rich relations. US servicemen were much better paid than the British and they had PX stores (military shops with goods shipped in from America) full of endless supplies of chocolates and chewing gum.

Americans were always surrounded by kids yelling, 'Got any gum, chum?'

To which the fast reply was, 'Gotta sister, mister?'

Spotting a chance for good public relations, the USAF laid on 379 parties for over 50,000 British children between July 1942 and July 1944.

OPERATION JERICHO

BATTLE BRIEFING

Resistance

In 1940 France fell to Nazi invaders after only six weeks of fighting. For some French people this was too much to bear and Resistance groups sprang up all over the country. Operating undercover, these freedom fighters hit back against the German army of occupation. They rescued shot-down aircrew and helped them escape to Britain, spied for the Allies, supplying information about German forces, and even sabotaged troop trains. If caught, they faced imprisonment in concentration camps or execution.

Invasion Threatened

By late 1943 there was a terrible crisis. The Allies were planning to invade, landing on the Normandy coast. The British and Americans needed the eyes, ears and fighting spirit of

82

the Resistance more than ever. The Germans knew an invasion was coming and were equally determined to stamp out any secret armies behind their lines. They set up a force of collaborators, other French people prepared to seek out and betray those fighting for freedom. By the winter of 1943–44 this plan was so successful that a member of the Resistance was lucky to survive six months without being arrested and shot. The lingering bitterness caused by collaboration still troubles France today.

The Allies were particularly worried about the situation in northern France around the town of Amiens. They needed all

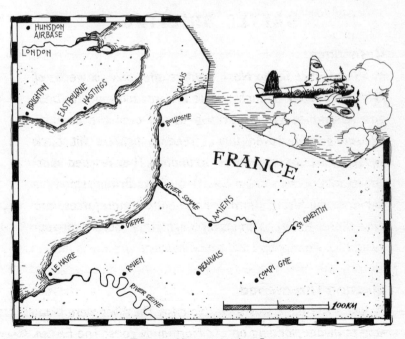

The town of Amiens in northern France.

83

the information they could get on the menacing V1 flying bomb sites (see chapter 6). If these missiles were fired in large numbers at Britain, then the invasion itself might be held up – or even abandoned. Yet so many people had been arrested that the Resistance network was on the point of collapse. Among them were key fighters such as the young and brave Jean Beaurin. Jean had led daring raids against the railways and blown up five troop trains, killing and injuring thousands of Germans and destroying their tanks and vehicles. At the beginning of 1944 the grim cells of Amiens prison were packed with 700 prisoners who, if tortured, might give away others. And worse, on 19 February, over a hundred were to be executed.

The Resistance had one unbreakable rule: if comrades were caught, the others had to try to save them. But, already weakened, how could they break into a heavily guarded prison and rescue so many? Their leader, Dominique Ponchardier, turned to Britain for help. Plans of the prison, the defences and the duty rosters of the guards were gathered at great risk and sent to London. Dominique also sent a daunting message. Could the RAF burst open Amiens prison and free the prisoners? Once they were out, Resistance teams would be waiting to hide them. If not, could the bombers destroy the prison? It was better for captured comrades to die than give away others.

PRISON BUSTERS

Basil Embry's Dilemma

The Amiens problem was dropped in the lap of Air Vice Marshall Basil Embry, a pint-sized ball of energy who made bigger men quake. Basil was Commander of 2 Group – twelve squadrons equipped with Mosquitoes, the fastest fighter-bombers flown by the Allies. Among his exploits was a daring escape from France in 1940. Captured after his plane was shot down, Basil killed his guards and crossed the Pyrenees to Spain – with the help of a Resistance group. He owed the French a personal favour.

Yet even Basil was dismayed by this mission. It would be easy enough to blast the prison to rubble, he thought, but to damage it just enough to allow a mass break-out? Now that was a tall order. Calling together his planning group, he shared his dilemma: 'We know, and so do those who have asked us to try and do this, that no matter how precise the bombing, many prisoners are liable to be killed too. I'm assured they accept this fact and therefore so must we.'

Like Joshua in the Bible, 2 Group had to bring the walls of Amiens prison tumbling down. It was little wonder then that the mission was named 'Operation Jericho'. With barely a month to go, the 'backroom boys' worked out every painstaking detail at breakneck speed. If they got it wrong, the Resistance fighters would pay with their lives.

Operation Jericho

The Target

Amiens prison was built on the outskirts of the town, next to the main road from Albert. It was a cross-shaped three-storey building, surrounded by a 20 ft (6 m) high perimeter wall. The prisoners were held in the longer arm of the cross, with the guards housed in extensions at each end. If the weather was clear, the Route d'Albert pointed to the target like a giant arrow. To focus thinking, a scale model gave a pilot's eye view of the prison from four miles away. This was made by 2 Group model shop, using aerial photographs and plans supplied by the Resistance. It became the centre of intense briefings as tactics were thrashed out.

Model of Amiens prison used to brief the Mosquito crews.

Timing

The raid was set to go any day from 10 February onwards – on the first fine day. But their time of arrival was crucial. It had to be noon. At midday the guards gathered in their mess hall for lunch – sitting targets! Wipe them out and the whole escape became much simpler. The streets too would be quiet, lessening the chance of killing innocent civilians.

The Leader

Group Captain Percy Pickard was to lead the attack. Better known as 'Pick' to his aircrews, he was a reluctant hero, a gentle giant who never wanted to kill anyone. But he had soon proved that he was good – very good at war. Like Basil, he too owed a debt to the French. On 24 February 1943 he had made a secret landing in a remote area. He had flown in at night to drop agents and supplies for the Resistance. His plane bogged down and almost everyone in the local village, including the police, worked furiously to pull the aircraft free. As he took off the Gestapo were already closing in. Tragically, some of those who helped him were caught.

The Men and the Machines

Mosquito fighter-bombers, 'Mossies', were the best planes for low-level, precision bombing. And this was a roof-top attack – the planes had to zoom in at 240 mph (385 kph), only 10 feet (3 m) above the ground. If the pilots released their bombs too soon, too high or too fast, there was a good chance they would bounce right over the target.

Basil picked the three squadrons of 140 Wing, based at Hunsdon, near London, for the Amiens mission. They were amongst his most experienced pilots and had spent the winter blitzing flying bomb sites. Eighteen planes, six from each squadron, would attack in three waves.

No. 487 Squadron, New Zealanders, had two objectives:

- Blast holes in the east and north sides of the perimeter wall. If only one side was breached the guards might be able to seal the gap with vehicles or machine-guns.
- Score a direct hit on the mess hall to kill and injure as many guards as possible. With luck, the survivors would be too confused to stop the breakout.

No. 464 Squadron, Australians, had the most delicate task of all:

- Blow the main building to make holes large enough for the prisoners to escape. The shock from the explosions should also shake open the cell doors.

No. 21 Squadron, British, drew the short straw. They had to stand off and watch the attack. If the raid failed to crack open the prison, 'Pick' would call them in to destroy it!

By the morning of Friday, 18 February even the steel nerves of Basil Embry were beginning to fray. For over a week the weather had been atrocious across Europe. Blizzards had swept the airfield and snow blanketed the ground. Even a kite would have had trouble getting aloft. But time had run out. The prisoners would be shot tomorrow. It was now or never.

The crews were called in for briefing and the final call, left to Group Captain Pickard. Pick studied the latest forecast. There would be no improvement over Britain, but there was a chance of clear skies over France. With two hours to the deadline he made the decision to go.

Two hours – a lifetime of waiting for the airmen. Jericho was tricky. It was almost certain there would be casualties. To ease tension the banter flew thick and fast:

'If you stare at those pin-ups any longer, you'll go blind.'

'Don't forget your life jacket – it helps the rescue teams find your body.'

Breakfast helped – an endless supply of fried eggs, strictly rationed for civilians. After that a brief time to relax – billiards, the Glenn Miller orchestra on the radio, reading, letter-writing to girlfriends or wives – just in case! Soon the mess was a fug of tobacco smoke.

Outside, the ground crews were in a flurry of activity. Engineers and electricians tested and retested systems; engines were run up and exhaust smoke drifted across

Group Captain Percy Pickard (left) and Flight Lieutenant Bill Broadly (right)
get ready for take-off on the Amiens raid.

the airfield; trolley drivers trundled out the 500 lb (225 kg) bombs; armourers prepared the ammunition belts, feeding them carefully into their narrow boxes. And still the unforgiving snow pelted down.

By 10:30 everyone was at dispersal, waiting for the final word. Surely in this weather it was impossible? Then Pick roared up, wound down the window of his car and yelled, 'Time, gentlemen, please.' Shuffling out in their thick flying boots the crews piled into trucks for the short run to the 'Mossies'. Once aboard the exhaustive cockpit drill began:

'Check petrol-cocks.'

'Petrol-cocks SET.'

'Check booster-pumps.'

'Booster-pumps ON.'

Like priest and congregation, pilot and navigator said their responses, as if reciting a fervent prayer. And in a way they were. This was their final, life-saving inspection of the plane. From engines to oxygen, if there was a fault, please let it show now.

Visibility Nil

With Merlins roaring, the Mosquitoes taxied to the downwind side of the airfield and lined up in pairs. At intervals of 100 yards (90 m) they took off from east to west. Throttles open, the aircraft tore down the runway, hugging the ground until they reached safety speed, 170 mph. By a little after 11:00 the last of the raiders was airborne. But the Mossies were climbing into the worst conditions the crews had ever known.

At 100 feet (30 m) above the runway visibility was nil. Dick Sugden of 464 Squadron recalled: 'We never saw anyone else. It was like flying in a blancmange.' Blind, the navigators used compass, map and ground radar to head for Littlehampton and the rendezvous with an escort of Typhoon fighters. Soon, four aircraft had lost their way, crews straining to see through snow-spattered canopies. As the minutes ticked by, they realized bitterly that they would arrive too late. Since timing was vital, one by one they turned for home. Not yet over France and a quarter of the strike force was gone!

As Dick Sugden neared Littlehampton (he hoped) the cloud suddenly cleared. There was the sea ahead of them, gleaming in the sun. And there was another Mossie breaking cloud and swerving right in front of them!

Dick heaved on the control column and almost cartwheeled his plane to avoid a smash. The plane juddered fiercely and seemed ready to tear apart.

'Get out of it, you idiot,' he yelled over the radio.

As the other plane wheeled urgently away Dick glimpsed its Id letter. 'God,' he thought, 'It's "F" for Freddy – Pick's plane'. Gulping he remembered the CO's last words at the briefing: 'I want complete radio silence. If any fool opens his mouth up there he'll be off my station tonight.'

Not only had Dick disobeyed, he had done so to curse Pick himself. But at least they hadn't collided!

They're Here

In Amiens prison Jean Beaurin stood at the small window of his cell. News of the RAF raid had been smuggled into the jail and each day since he had anxiously scanned the sky. In the distance a church bell dolefully tolled noon as if marking a funeral – his own. Yet as the bell faded, air raid sirens ripped the air. In the distance he could hear the throb of aircraft engines. 'Get down,' he yelled to his cellmates. 'They're here.'

It had been a spectacular trip. The Mosquitoes had skimmed over the channel at over 300 mph, their propeller tips barely 15 feet above the sea. They had hoped to duck under the German radar, but the powerful Wurzburg sets had detected them. Soon the run to Amiens became a series of doglegs designed to fool enemy fighter controllers and side-step anti-aircraft batteries. Ten minutes from the target, Q for Queenie, flown by 'Tich' Hanafin, was caught by flak. He turned for home badly wounded, the Mossie limping on one engine. Meanwhile, only a few kilometres from the target, the 'Abbeville Boys', the toughest Luftwaffe unit in France, were ordered to stand by for immediate take-off.

At 12:03 the first wave of Mosquitoes from 487 Squadron swept in along the Route d'Albert. They were so low that section leader 'Black' Smith had to watch his wings didn't clip the telegraph poles. Suddenly the prison appeared, standing out like a grey castle in the bleak winter landscape. 'It looks just like the briefing model,' yelled Pilot Officer Sparkes.

The last minute passed in a blur of concentration. Open bomb doors ... check course ... forty seconds ... thirty seconds ... twenty seconds ... steady ... speed – 240 mph ... height – 10 feet ... BOMBS GONE ... now hard on the stick ... clear the wall ... leapfrog the roof.

To French civilians diving for cover, it seemed as if the crazy RAF were trying to ram the prison.

The second wave, 464 Squadron, had a problem. Section leader Bob Iredale got a blunt warning from his

Mosquitoes attacking Amiens prison.

navigator: 'We're bang on time, but the first lot weren't. If we follow them in without a two-minute gap, it won't be healthy.'

Bob knew what he meant. The bombs dropped by 487 Squadron had delayed action fuses – go in too quickly and they might be caught in the blast. Swinging to port, the Aussies began a holding circuit to gain time – a circuit that took them over Amiens-Glisy Luftwaffe base. Dense flak burst around the Mosquitoes and they could see enemy pilots racing for their planes. Circling back over the Albert Road they dropped into the same low-level attack pattern.

To make up for the lost planes, the 464 boys hit the target in two sections of two. Bob and his wingman released their bombs at 12:05 precisely. The last strikes came seconds later from Ian McRitchie and Group Captain Pickard. In those two hectic minutes of combat, the pilots only caught glimpses of the damage they had inflicted. But one disturbing impression came through – the plans had gone awry. 'Black' Smith had watched his bombs smash through the perimeter wall without exploding. The 464 Mossies had seen other unexploded bombs bouncing and skipping in the prison yard. It was clear that the perimeter wall had been far weaker than anyone expected while the bombs, dropped from such a low height, had gone skidding in all directions when they hit thick ice.

Amiens prison wreathed in smoke and dust.

What happened next was up to Pick. The CO had acted as 'Tail-end Charlie' for the mission – the last plane to attack. This was deliberate. With his bombs gone, Pick climbed to 500 ft (150 m) to circle the prison and assess the success of the raid. Through the smoke pall he had to make sense out of the chaos. Hundreds of lives rested on his next decision. Should he call in 21 Squadron to pound the jail – or send them home?

As Pick circled a picture came together. The guards' building had taken a direct hit; the perimeter walls had gaping holes; the main prison had been hit at the junction of the north and west wings. Crucially, dozens of men in what looked like overalls were scampering over the ruins – some of the prisoners at least were out. In spite of the wayward bombs Jericho had worked. Pick's voice came over the RT. He was shouting, 'RED DADDY! RED DADDY!' The others breathed a sigh of relief. This was the signal for 21 Squadron to turn back to Britain.

It was the last anyone heard from poor Pick ...

The Cost

The flight back became a running fight. Fw 190s and Me 109s dived repeatedly on the fleeing Mossies. Most of these screaming assaults were driven off by the escort of Typhoon fighters but others cut their way through. Several Mossies were shot up but gamely they stayed in the air. Then there was the flak. German anti-aircraft gunners were renowned for their accuracy. The dash to the coast became a rat run through dozens of flak batteries.

Ian McRitchie made it to Dieppe, with the Channel in sight, when suddenly his plane lifted in the air like a toy. A gun battery had found his range and kept pumping shells into his stricken plane. He was hit. His navigator sat dead beside him. Ian barely had the strength left to make a crash-landing in a field, where he was quickly captured.

If Pick had a fault it was too much courage. He took chances and expected them to come off. In his adventures fortune really had favoured the brave – but that Friday he let the odds become too high. Once Pick had given the all-clear to 21 Squadron, he should have followed the golden rule: 'Get out of there.' But he didn't. He circled the prison again and again, waiting for the smoke and dust to settle – waiting for a last clear view. By the time he swung F for Freddy away it was too late. Pick was bounced by two of the Abbeville 190s. In a desperate dogfight he mauled one Focke-Wulf badly enough to drive it off. But the other swung in and shot his whole tailplane off. The Mossie flipped over on its back and dived, the impact on hitting the ground scattering wreckage for hundreds of yards. Pick and his navigator, Bill Broadly, died instantly.

In Amiens there was mayhem. Many German guards were dead and over 250 prisoners had escaped. This was better than the Resistance had dared hope for. In the

The damaged prison buildings, looking from a breach
in the west outer wall.

coming months they regrouped and reorganized. When
the invasion force hit the beaches on 6 June the Free
French forces helped to bring the Amiens region to a
standstill.

Yet in war there is no such thing as an easy victory.
Around 40 prisoners were killed in the raid as well as
innocent civilians in nearby houses. A German military
hospital was also hit and over 50 soldiers killed. During
April the Nazis shot 260 survivors of the raid, some
who had not escaped and others who had been recaptured. Their bodies were dumped in a mass grave in a
ditch at Arras.

FIGHTING FACTS

The Marvellous Mosquito

Would you like to go to war in an unarmed wooden bomber, held together by glue?

Say that again – UNARMED? WOODEN?? GLUE???

Not keen? Neither was the British government when the de Havilland Aircraft Company first suggested the idea in 1938. 'Stresses from the engines will tear it apart,' experts at the Air Ministry said. Luckily for Britain they soon admitted they were wrong. By the end of the war, 6,710 de Havilland 'Mosquitoes' had been built in the UK, Canada and Australia.

In today's high-tech weapons speak, the Mosquito would be called 'a multi-role combat aircraft'. It became one of the most versatile planes of World War II, serving as a bomber, fighter-bomber, fighter, night-fighter, photo-reconnaissance plane, ship and submarine buster.

'The Wooden Wonder'

RAF crew loved the 'Mossie' and nicknamed it the 'Wooden Wonder'. So what made it so good?

Material

A wooden plane sounds like something from World War I, not World War II. In fact the idea was brilliant. Since the Mosquito was the only all-wooden British plane, it was not in competition with other aircraft for scarce metals, especially aluminium.

Labour

The Mosquito was built by people with woodworking skills – furniture manufacturers, shop fitters, coach and caravan builders. This meant Britain was making good use of all its workers at a time when there was a desperate shortage of labour.

Construction

The fuselage was made in two halves from a sandwich of birch plywood, filled with lightweight balsa wood. This composite construction gave it great strength. The wings were made from overlapping laminated planks of spruce. Many parts were built by small firms all over the country and sent to the de Havilland factories at Hatfield and Leavesden for final assembly. Even better, if a Mosquito crash-landed or was hit by enemy fire, it was easier to repair than a metal plane.

Speed

Although planned as a bomber, the Mosquito was designed like a fighter, to keep drag to a minimum. Lightweight and powered by two Merlin engines the Mossie was as fast as any German piston-engined fighter, even the awesome Fw 190 (see table).

Armament

The bomber version could carry a load up to 4,000 lb (1,814 kg), the same as the much larger Flying Fortress. Remarkably, the bombers carried no weapons. The whole point of the design, de Havilland argued, was to save weight, drag and crew numbers, making the Mosquito fast enough to outrun any trouble.

Fighter-bomber versions, like those in Operation Jericho, were fitted with four .303 machine-guns in the nose and four 20 mm cannon under the cockpit. Fired together, these had the impact of a three-ton truck hitting a brick wall at 50 mph.

Crew

The Mossie only had two crewmen, the pilot and navigator. The navigator had a busy time – as well as guiding the aircraft he had to act as bomb-aimer and radio operator. Smooth teamwork was the key to success. Pilot and navigator often became close friends.

Mosquito vs. Focke-Wulf

Type	Max. Speed	Range	Weapons	Comment
Mosquito FB Mk VI	385 mph (620 kph) at 13,000 ft (3,960 m)	1,650 miles (2,655 km) with 2,000 lb of bombs	Four 20 mm cannon and four .303 inch machine-guns.	The Mossie was a winner in every role it was given.
Focke-Wulf 190 A-5	402 mph (645 kph) at 18,000 ft (5,485 m)	500 miles (805 km)	Two 7.9 mm machine-guns and four 20 mm cannon.	The best German fighter of the war.

VENGEANCE
WEAPON

BATTLE BRIEFING

First Strike

On 6 June 1944 Allied armies stormed ashore at Normandy
– and Londoners began to relax. For months German
air raids had been sporadic and light. Now, with the invasion
of Europe underway, it seemed possible that the war might be
over by Christmas. This new confidence was rudely shattered
at 04.25 on Tuesday, 13 June when the sirens wailed again.

A little earlier, at 04.08, two Observer Corps volunteers at
Dymchurch on Romney Marsh watched in amazement as a
German missile roared across the sky towards them. They
had been warned to look out for a new secret weapon, but it
still came as a shock – small, slim and very fast, with a weird
engine noise like a 'Model T Ford going up a hill'. They had
made the first official sighting of a V1 flying bomb.

No one can be sure if it was the same missile that reached

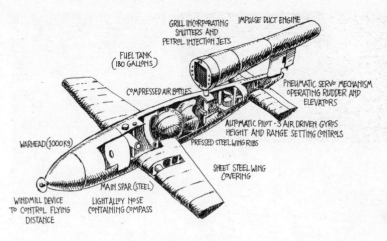

GRILL INCORPORATING
SHUTTERS AND
PETROL INJECTION JETS

IMPULSE DUCT ENGINE

FUEL TANK
(180 GALLONS)

COMPRESSED AIR BOTTLES

PNEUMATIC SERVO MECHANISM
OPERATING RUDDER AND
ELEVATORS

AUTOMATIC PILOT - 3 AIR DRIVEN GYROS
HEIGHT AND RANGE SETTING CONTROLS

PRESSED STEEL WING RIBS

WARHEAD (1000 Kg)

SHEET STEEL WING
COVERING

WINDMILL DEVICE
TO CONTROL FLYING
DISTANCE

MAIN SPAR (STEEL)

LIGHT ALLOY NOSE
CONTAINING COMPASS

A V1 flying bomb.

London, since four were sighted that dawn. Three crashed harmlessly, but one stuttered to a halt over Bethnal Green.

A ten-year-old girl remembered: 'The engine stopped, then there was the sound of whistling ... and the next thing was a tremendous bang and the front room windows came in.'

She escaped, but six people died and over 200 were made homeless. This was the first of 2,242 V1s to hit London in the coming weeks, killing 5,126 civilians and seriously injuring 14,712.

The V1 was the first of Hitler's high-tech terror weapons, a last gamble to force the British out of the war. The idea to develop a pilotless, jet-engined bomb was given the go-ahead in 1942. It was code-named Fi 103, after the Fiesler aircraft company that was to make the missile. Development took place at the Peenemunde rocket research station on the

103

One of the first targets,
Lewisham High Street, 1944.

Baltic coast, with the first test launch on 24 December. On 8 November, however, a British spotter plane flying over Peenemunde photographed an experimental launch ramp with a V1 ready for take-off. This was the start of a deadly race between Germany and Britain. The Nazis pushed the V1 programme ahead as quickly as possible while British air raids caused endless delays.

When the first flying bombs were fired at England that invasion summer, they were a year late and RAF Fighter Command was ready and waiting ...

REVENGE!

On 16 April 1944 Joseph Goebbels, Hitler's Minister of **Propaganda**, broadcast to the hard-pressed German people. For those living miserably in the ruins of heavily bombed towns he had a message of hope:

It will not be long before the British will have to show the same steadiness as the Germans. We have the hardest part of the war behind us. England has it still in front of her.

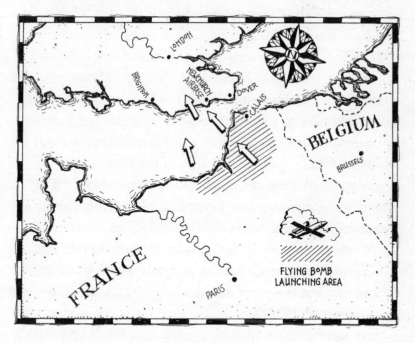

Flight path of the VIs.

Many listeners were puzzled. What did he mean? It was over two years since the glorious days of the Luftwaffe blitz on Britain and six months since Hitler himself had promised revenge for British and American air raids. Was this another worthless Nazi lie, like the boasts about victory at Stalingrad? Or could there be some truth in the rumours of *Vergeltungswaffen* – 'Reprisal weapons'?

Although Goebbels was fit to burst with excitement, the public could not be told how true the gossip was. The first secret weapon, the V1 flying bomb, was almost ready for use. In France over 60 launch sites, hidden in woods across the Pas de Calais, set their target as London. Soon the endless delays and cancellations would be over. Soon these deadly pilotless planes would bring revenge! But would they, the Minister wondered, come in time to save Germany from defeat?

Open Fire

Colonel Max Wachtel, commanding officer of Flak (anti-aircraft) Regiment 155 (W), was one of the men on whom Nazi hopes depended. Goebbels was well aware that this unit had nothing to do with anti-aircraft guns. The title was part of their cover. Flak Regiment 155 (W) was the covert (secret) force that would fire the V1s.

However, Max was a worried man. His concerns had nothing to do with his troops. They were first-class soldiers and engineers who had risked their lives to train with the new weapons. He ruefully remembered that the first VIs had been more likely to explode near their launch ramps than reach their targets. No, his men had proved their skill and courage. But almost everything else continued to go wrong.

Allied bombing had badly disrupted the flying bomb factories. The first missiles should have rolled off the production lines in August 1943, rising to a total of 5,000 bombs a month by April 1944. Instead only a trickle of bombs had been made by February 1944 and barely a thousand left the factories in April. Each bomb carried an 850 kg payload, but in such small numbers they would barely disrupt, let alone smash, a city the size of London.

Equally maddening were the air attacks on the missile sites. The tiny bases were built in remote areas, but even so, British aerial photographs had given most of them away. Once located, the concrete launch ramps, blast walls and blockhouses made distinctive targets.

Preparing a VI for launch.

Since December 1943 Allied bombers had rained explosives on every suspect site from Calais to Dieppe. These raids had cost the British and Americans dear – 154 planes and 771 aircrew were dead or missing by the end of May. But their lives had not been wasted. Eighty-two of Max's 96 launch sites had been knocked out or smashed.

Faced with disaster, Max had risen to the challenge. Repairs were carried out to the damaged bases and new ones begun. What's more, he made sure that there was more than enough construction work to be spotted and bombed! No, he hadn't cracked under the strain. It was all part of a brilliant deception plan.

Elsewhere, hidden from Allied spotter planes in dense woods, smaller sites had been rushed ahead. This time only the foundations were laid, waiting for the last-minute delivery of launch ramp kits. These sites would not become operational until days, or perhaps hours, before they were used. Inevitably a few had been discovered and air raids had ripped them apart, but most remained camouflaged and undamaged. In spite of the odds, by June 1944, Flak Regiment 155 was almost ready to strike back.

Almost, but not quite! On 6 June, the invasion began and Hitler demanded that the VIs be unleashed at once. Germany was now faced with a war on two fronts, the British and Americans in the West and the Russians in the East. Max and his men worked themselves to the point of bleary-eyed exhaustion to obey, but once again enemy air power forced delays. To support the attack in Normandy, Allied bombers blasted anything that moved. Rail and road traffic ground to a halt and with it the supply of VIs, ramps and fuel.

Finally, shortly after 03:30 on 13 June, Flak Regiment 155 opened fire. Each VI roared in anger, locked in the firing trolley to the launch ramp. Then as the jet engine developed sufficient thrust, it was catapulted free and soared into the air. Yet this wasn't the knock-out blow that Max had dreamed of months ago. Instead, only ten flying bombs lifted off and of those only one reached London. Pathetic, but a start! In the coming days the bombardment increased, until by the end of June dozens of VIs were launched each day. As Hitler and Goebbels had vowed, the British faced a new terror.

Tempest in the Skies

If Max and Flak Regiment 155 enjoyed a sense of triumph, it was not to last long. In Britain others were waiting to protect London. In the front line against the flying bombs were the three squadrons of 150 Wing, led by air ace Roland Beamont – 'Bee' to his friends.

Bee had already seen plenty of action. He had fought in the Battle of France and the Battle of Britain in 1940 and flown night-fighters against German bombers in 1941. In 1942–43 he had led daring sweeps over occupied Europe and his attacks on railways earned him a new nickname, 'Train Buster Beamont'. In February 1944 he was appointed Wing Commander of 150 Wing to oversee a special project, re-equipping two squadrons with a top secret plane. This was the sensational Hawker Tempest V. With a top speed of about 435 mph (700 kph) it became the fastest piston-engined fighter of the war below 20,000 ft (6,100 m). Rugged, easy to fly and with a fine gun platform, it was Bee's favourite plane. The Wing was trained and ready just in time to cover the D-Day invasion. And just in time to tackle the VIs.

Bee had chosen Newchurch, on Romney Marsh in Kent, as his Wing base. The airfield was rough and ready, but in the right place, smack in the middle of the flying bomb flight path to London. This was fine for catching VIs, but made life on the ground risky. Shrapnel often rained down over the airfield, puncturing the tents where pilots and ground crew slept. As luck would have it, the unit's first casualty was caused by a friendly plane. A passing P47 Thunderbolt fired on a flying bomb and a stray bullet drilled a hole through the hand of a sleeping airman.

Flying Bomb Battle

On the evening of 15 June, 150 Wing was warned to expect an imminent attack on London. The new German weapon was code-named 'Diver' – a small, pilotless plane, streaking in at 400 mph (640 kph) and at heights of up to 5,000 ft (1,525 m). At dawn the next day the first 'Diver' alert came over the telephone and the Wing scrambled into a grey and drizzly sky.

Soon after take-off radar control directed Bee and his wingman, Bob Cole, to intercept a missile south-east of Folkestone. In spite of clear directions, cloud and sheeting rain cloaked the V1.

'Target is closing rapidly to your port side,' intoned the calm voice of the controller.

Heatedly Bee peered round and pulled his Tempest in a tight turn to port. Where was it? At that moment he glimpsed a small, dark shape flit though a break in the cloud below. The chase was on.

Diving at full power, the Tempests levelled out in hot pursuit of the flying bomb. Bee estimated it was doing about 370 mph but, at 410 mph, he was gaining fast. He looked at it with fascination − a tiny grey monoplane with a glowing, smoke-blackened jet engine at the back. So this was the new face of war? Not the courage and skill of pilot against pilot, instead he was hunting a robot bomb at whirlwind speed.

As they crossed the coast Bee closed in. At 400 yards (365 m) he opened fire with his four 20 mm Hispano cannon − and missed completely. At 300 yards (275 m) he fired again and hit the port wing. No effect! Third time lucky? At 200 yards he raked the fuselage and engine until his ammunition was exhausted. And watched in dismay as the cannon shells seemed to bounce off.

Was the blasted thing invulnerable? Then the engine of the VI cut out and it immediately lost speed.

Thank God! They could be stopped.

Bee called in Bob to finish the job. A long blast from the wingman's cannon rolled the missile on its back. It dived into a field near Maidstone and exploded, a goldfish bowl shock wave rippling outwards.

When they returned to base to refuel and rearm, Bee and Bob reported their kill. Buzzing with excitement they asked if it was the first. Gallingly for 150 Wing, they had been beaten by an hour. A Mosquito night-fighter, flown by Flight Lieutenant Musgrave, had claimed the record. Still, there was no time to be disappointed. Since dawn over 50 VIs had been tracked and more were coming in. Within minutes the pair were scrambled again.

By the end of 16 June the Wing had downed eleven missiles, an amazing achievement against an unknown and sinister enemy. That night, in hectic mission reports, experiences were shared and tactics thrashed out. One thing was clear – these steel-cased VIs were tough nuts to shoot down. Pilots had to get in close.

Guns were re-set so that their fire harmonized (converged or met) 200 yards (182 m) ahead, much nearer than Fighter Command approved. This was risky. No one could be certain that an attacking aircraft would survive if a VI blew up at that range. The answer came the next afternoon when a blackened Tempest landed. The elevators were charred and part of the rudder burned away. The shocked pilot reported:

> The sky was overcast, but there was a big ray of sunshine coming through a hole in the clouds. A V1 broke out in front of me. I was right underneath it and let fly for two or three seconds. When I was only 50 yards (15 m) away, it blew up in my face. My wingman saw me disappear in a sheet of flame and shouted, 'You are on fire. Bale out!' I thought I had had it.

Amazingly, both pilot and plane survived.

Soon Bee suffered the same wild ride, 400 mph through the middle of an 850 kg bomb explosion. On 21 June, he described it to an awe-struck reporter:

> You can see the cannon-strikes on the bomb and a few flashes. Then suddenly the whole sky goes black and red and you duck. Everyone who has blown up a winged bomb at short range finds himself on his back when he comes out the other side, probably because the pilot goes through a complete vacuum which turns his aeroplane upside down.

The close kill tactic had been proved a success, but it didn't work every time. In the next six weeks eighteen fighters were badly damaged and six pilots killed when V1s blew up in the air.

Clearing the field

In the coming days other difficulties had to be solved and Bee had firm views about what should happen.

Problem

Radar control could only get fighters to within half a mile (0.8 km) of a flying bomb. After this, detection was down to sharp eyes and luck. Too much time was lost in poor weather.

Solution

Station Observer Corps posts at half-mile intervals along the coast from Eastbourne to Folkestone. Observers to fire distress rockets towards any V1 they spot. This will give pilots a useful clue to the direction of the incoming missile.

Problem

Only a handful of aircraft types stood a chance of catching a V1 – the Tempest V, Spitfires IX and XIV, Mustang IIIs and Mosquitoes. Yet the skies seemed as busy as at an airshow with too many older and slower planes taking pot-shots at V1s. And getting in the way!

Solution

Ban all other aircraft from the interception area and leave the hunting to the experts – 150 Wing and a few others, like the fearless Poles of 316 'City of Warsaw' Squadron.

Bee flew to Uxbridge, the HQ of No. 11 Group and requested immediate action on these solutions. The

Commander-in-Chief listened carefully and agreed. If he had any doubts they were soon put to rest. With the skies cleared Beamont's boys could get on with the job. The interception rate shot up almost at once.

For the next six weeks 150 Wing fought a hectic battle against the VIs. Pilots flew four or five sorties a day, living and eating by their planes. In normal combat they expected to fly for 500–600 hours a month, but that June and July they were operational for 900–1,000 hours. The pressure was intense and affected ground crews too. The Tempest was a marvellous aircraft, but it was powered by the temperamental Napier Sabre engine. It was common for fitters to work eighteen hours a day to keep the squadrons in the air. Yet in spite of all leave being cancelled, morale was high. The reason was simple – Bee was a fearless and popular leader. Men rose to the challenges he set them.

By early August Wing Commander Beamont's 'personal bag' of VIs stood at 30. Inspired by his example, 150 Wing had destroyed 632 missiles, the top-scoring RAF unit by far. The VI threat was not over, but the worst had passed. Allied troops began to overrun the launch sites and by early September Flak Unit 155 had pulled back to Holland. London was now out of range of ground-launched flying bombs. It was time for the Tempests to move on to Belgium and the air war in Europe.

FIGHTING FACTS

Every extra mile counts

During V1 tests in Germany, Hitler was shown a dazzling display – a flying bomb easily outrunning a captured Spitfire Mark V. It gave the German leader the impression that the V1 would be unstoppable. But British aircraft technology did not stand still. By June 1944 a number of piston-engined planes, like the Tempest and Spitfire XIV, were fast enough to catch the jet-engined missiles – but only just. Every extra mile per hour that could be teased from them was vital and a number of ingenious modifications were made. Ground crew followed urgent DIY instructions:

How to soup-up your fighter

- Polish all surfaces until as smooth as mirrors to reduce drag.
- Strip off all surplus weight, including layers of paint. V1s can't fire back so remove cockpit armour (usually behind seats to protect pilots from enemy fire).
- Adapt engines to run on 150 octane fuel and increase boost to give extra power.

Although results varied, many planes gained an extra 30 mph (40 kph).

Tip the Wing

On 23 June 1944 a Spitfire pilot tried a new and rash method of dealing with a V1. He flew alongside the missile and according to the official RAF history 'threw the flying bomb on its back by tipping it with his wing so that it fell out of control'. News soon spread and every hotshot pilot was keen to have a go. One Pole of 316 Squadron successfully flipped the wing of a V1, only to

A Spitfire tips a V1 over.

watch in horror as it rolled back and snapped the end off his own light alloy wing. He made a hasty but safe landing.

Jet vs. Jet

The Germans were ahead of the British in the development of jet engine technology, but only by a narrow margin. In May 1941 the first British test plane, the Gloucester E28/39, was flown and the first operational jet, the Gloucester Meteor, went into service with 616

Squadron in July 1944. The Meteor caught the public imagination and many thought that the flying bomb bombardment was beaten by this new wonder plane. In fact the Meteors arrived too late to make much difference and only shot down thirteen VIs.

Buzz Bombs and Doodlebugs

The jet engine of the VI had an eerie sound. Once heard it was never forgotten. Witnesses described in different, vivid ways:

- 'a train trundling over a wooden bridge';
- 'a sinister grunting';
- 'a washing machine';
- 'a cough, clattering, like a diesel truck';
- 'a load of biscuit tins rattling'.

This peculiar engine note led to the British nicknames for the VI – the 'doodlebug' or the 'buzz bomb'.

A Terrifying Silence

The British people soon learned that while a VI puttered its noisy way across the sky, they were safe. The danger came when the engine cut out. Flying bombs were loaded with only enough fuel to reach their target. When this ran out, the engine failed and the missile dived. Civilians described a 'dreadful silence' that lasted about twelve seconds – the time from the engine stopping to the VI exploding.

VI Data

- 6,725 VIs reached England.
- 2,242 landed in London.
- 1,444 landed in Kent.
- 1,772 shot down by fighters:
    - 638 by Tempests
    - 428 by Mosquitoes
    - 303 by Spitfire XIVs
    - 232 by Mustangs
    - 158 by slower fighters – Typhoons, Spitfire Vs, IXs or XII.
- 1,460 shot down by anti-aircraft guns.
- 231 were caught by barrage balloons.
- Altogether 51.5 per cent of VIs spotted by the defences were destroyed.
- 6,184 civilians were killed and 17,981 injured.

Mysterious Gas Explosions

Hitler had worse in store for Londoners than the VI. At 18:43 on 8 September 1944 an explosion in Chiswick killed three people. As casualties mounted, a series of mysterious explosions were blamed on leaking gas mains. Such a pretence could not be kept up for long and in November, Winston Churchill admitted Britain was under attack by another German secret weapon, the V2. This time it was unstoppable.

The V2 was the forerunner of today's long range missiles. Powered by a rocket motor it soared up to

The supersonic V2.

110,000 ft (30,000 m), the edge of space, before diving at 3,600 mph (5,780 kph). No aircraft stood a chance of catching one. The V2 carried a 1,145 lb (975 kg) warhead. As many as 1,115 hit England, 517 in the London area, and 2,754 people were killed.

GLOSSARY

Blitzkrieg – 'lightning war'. The coordinated use of
   aircraft, tanks and infantry
Concentration camp – a Nazi prison camp
Dispersal – remote parts of the airfield where the planes
   could be spaced over a wide area in case they were
   attacked from the air
Fuselage – main body of the plane
Luftwaffe – the German air force
Michelin Man – fat rubber man used in tyre adverts
Morale – will to carry on (fighting), general spirits
Morphine – a pain-killing drug
Nacelle – section of the wing structure that held the
   engine
Propaganda – political advertising. Goebbels' job was
   to persuade the German people to accept the Nazi
   government's version of events, through film, radio
   and public speeches

Wingmen – the two pilots on either side of the leader in a V formation

ACKNOWLEDGEMENTS

Imperial War Museum: p.11 CH1170, p.12 C5655, p.20 CH15174, p.21 C1869, p.25 MH13647, p.51 HU35639, p.64 C4973, p.67 CH7774, p.86 C4742 p.90 CH14105, p.94 C4732, p.95 C4734, p.98 C4739, p.104 CH15109, p.107 CL3430, p.117 CH16281, p.120 CL3429

Thanks to George Tones for checking and changing the technical specifications of aircraft performance – a minefield for possible mistakes.

Every effort has been made to trace copyright holders. We would be grateful to hear from any copyright holders not acknowledged here.

WORLD WAR II
ON LAND

NEIL TONGE

INTRODUCTION

On 1 September 1939, Germany invaded Poland. Britain and France warned the German dictator, Adolf Hitler, to withdraw his troops from that country within two days; otherwise they would declare war on Germany.

Hitler had no reason to believe them. So far they had given in to every one of his demands. First the Rhineland, then Austria and finally Czechoslovakia. Now it was the turn of Poland.

But this time he was wrong. On 3 September Britain and France declared war on Germany. There was little these allies of Poland could do, however, for they were hundreds of miles away and separated by Germany itself. Poland stood little chance against Hitler's massed tanks and the country was overrun within six weeks.

Britain sent its small Expeditionary Force to fight along-side the French but for eight months neither side launched attacks against one another. It was as if they were not at war at all. This brief period of calm before the storm broke in 1940 is often called the 'Phoney War'.

Hitler, however, was merely waiting for the best moment to strike. In May 1940 the German army launched a surprise attack in the mountainous region of the Ardennes, where the Allies were least expecting it. British and French forces were pushed back to the beaches of Dunkirk in a matter of weeks. An armada of ships, from pleasure boats to battleships, set out from Britain to rescue the remnants of the Allied armies. Over 200,000 British and 100,000 French were plucked from the jaws of the German **panzers** and brought safely back to England. France surrendered shortly afterwards, and Britain was left to fight on alone during what became her darkest days.

Success followed success for Hitler – until he made the fatal mistake of invading Russia in 1941. At last, Britain had an ally against fascist Germany and Italy.

Then what had only been a European war was transformed into a world war. Mussolini, the fascist dictator of Italy, dreamed of recreating the Roman Empire and launched campaigns in the Balkans and North Africa. He had little success and Hitler had to come to the rescue by strengthening his forces with German troops.

Later that same year, Japan made a surprise attack on the American pacific fleet. As a consequence, America declared war on Japan. Germany came to the help of her Asian ally and declared war on America. Further defeats followed for the British in Asia. Their colonies of Hong Kong, Singapore, Malaya and Burma fell to the Japanese until their forces were hammering on the gates of British India itself. But India did not fall.

1942 saw the first glimmerings of hope for the Allies. Slowly the tide was turning in their favour. In 1942, General Erwin Rommel, the hero of the German army, was defeated at the battle of El Alamein and his army pushed out of North Africa. In Russia, whole German battalions perished in the bitter cold or at the hands of the Russian army. In the Far East, the Japanese were gradually pushed back across the Pacific, and from Burma, to their homeland.

By 1944 the fascist countries of Germany, Italy and Japan were clearly losing the war. A second front was opened in Europe when the Allied armies landed in Normandy, France in June 1944. But as the Allies neared the frontiers of Germany, enemy resistance stiffened. It was to be one full year before the Allies entered the ruins of Berlin to find Hitler had taken his own life. In the Far East, the dropping of atomic bombs on two Japanese cities in August forced the Japanese to surrender.

There were thousands of individuals caught up in these powerful and extraordinary events. This book captures the stories of six people who were part of the history of a world in flames.

• In 1940, Private Ernie Leggett is one of the gallant

band of British soldiers who bear the brunt of the German onslaught on France. Badly wounded, he fears he will never see his home again.

• In 1942 the German army is 40 miles away from Cairo, Egypt. Bill Norris takes charge of a delivery of new Sherman tanks. Will they be enough to defeat the German general, Erwin Rommel, and his victorious Africa Korps?

• Parachuted behind enemy lines into occupied France in 1943, will Pearl Witherington, a brave Resistance fighter, evade capture and torture by the Gestapo?

• In June 1944 6,000 Allied ships lie off the coast of Normandy. Amongst the invasion force, Sergeant-Major Stan Hollis waits to lead his men into battle.

• October 1944. The Allied plan to shorten the war has gone disastrously wrong. Dr Graeme Warrack, captured by the Germans, decides to make a bid for freedom.

• In 1944 the 'Forgotten Army' of Burma is caught in a life and death struggle against Japanese forces. Gurkha rifleman Lachhiman Gurung stands alone against overwhelming odds.

RETREAT
FROM HELL

BATTLE BRIEFING

On 1 September 1939 German forces attacked Poland, the ally of Great Britain and France. On 3 September, Neville Chamberlain, the British prime minister, warned the Germans to withdraw their army from Poland otherwise Britain and France would declare war. The Germans ignored this demand.

Cut off from Poland by Germany, there was little the Allies could do to help. The Polish army was no match for the lightning strikes of the German army. Polish cavalry made useless charges against German tanks. Heroically brave but badly equipped, they disintegrated within weeks and surrendered.

The Allies could have helped Poland by launching an attack in the west but very little happened. The British sent the BEF (British Expeditionary Force) of four divisions to join the 72 divisions of the French army but both armies needed to be trained and there was no plan for an invasion of

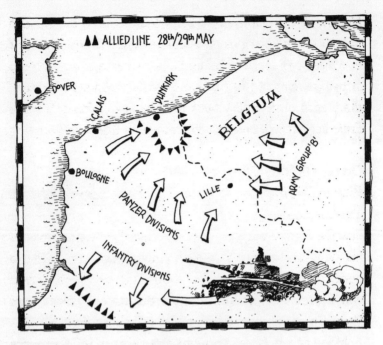

The Maginot Line.

Germany. Instead, they sheltered behind huge defence works called the Maginot Line, waiting for the Germans to destroy themselves on suicidal attacks at heavily defended positions.

At the end of the Polish campaign Hitler ordered his generals to prepare for an autumn attack against the Allies in the west. Bad weather and advice from his general, however, persuaded Hitler to change his mind and wait for the spring.

As dawn broke on 10 May 1940, the Germans unleashed their terror. Instead of attacking the Maginot Line they simply went around it. Drawing the Allied armies into Belgium and

Holland, their main thrust was further south in the wooded and hilly area known as the Ardennes. Spearheaded by tanks and dive-bombers, the German army sliced the Allied armies in two, sending the British Expeditionary Force and part of the French army reeling back to the coast of France. Private Ernie Leggett was amongst the retreating British soldiers.

Date: 10 May 1940 onwards
Place: Orchies, near Lille, northern France

A Sudden Awakening

Private Ernie Leggett pulled the blankets tightly round his neck and snuggled deeper into the warmth of the bed. 'No hurry to be up and about in this strange kind of war,' he thought to himself. 'Just the sort of soldiering I like – no shooting and lots of fun in la belle France.'

Most of his mates thought the same way. They were sick of the war before it had even started. They wanted to go home and did not give a bean for a faraway people in Poland and a strange-sounding city called Danzig. Besides, Ernie had heard someone say that it was all Germans that lived in the city anyway, so why the fuss? If only Hitler would stop stirring things up they could all go home.

Ernie turned on to his other side and stretched. 'May as well go home – not a German to be seen and all we do is march and drill all day long.' Glowing coals in the hearth and a singing kettle on the range filled Ernie's mind. He longed for home, for his little village of

Clippersby. And it was true. The tiny BEF and their French allies had done little more than stare at one other since September of last year.

A few pamphlets had been dropped on Germany warning them that they would lose the war, although it was difficult to see how this could be achieved with bits of paper. True, the French had advanced into Germany – all of five miles! And occasionally they fired a few rounds at the Germans from the safety of the Maginot Line. With the memory of 1.3 million men dead from the 1914–18 war fresh in every Frenchman's mind it was understandable that there was no enthusiasm to rush to war.

Without warning the door was nearly shaken from its hinges by a furious knock. Ernie, drifting back into sleep, was jolted awake. 'What the——?' he cursed as he pulled the blankets aside and peered outside. Company Sergeant Major Gristock was in the middle of the Rue de la Gare bellowing out instructions for the men to 'fall-in'.

Ernie tumbled out of the door, pulling his battledress jacket tight but leaving his shirt tail streaming out behind him. In the distance, he caught the sound of the muffled boom of heavy artillery fire coming from the direction of Lille. The sky was the usual steel-grey of early morning but at the airfield bases, less than ten miles away, the sky was glowing a smoky red and plumes of oily smoke were curling up into the sky.

One hundred and twenty men of the 2nd Battalion, Royal Norfolk Regiment, tumbled into the streets of Orchies where they had been billeted.

'Attention!' Sergeant Gristock barked out the command and seconds later every man had snapped to attention.

'Get your kits, we're moving out – NOW!'

Within minutes the men had grabbed their equipment, including one or two 'unofficial' bottles of wine. They were barely a mile from their billets when several black specks appeared in the morning light. Screaming from the sky, German bombers flew low over Orchies. Several muffled explosions could be heard as the bombs detonated and clouds of dusty smoke billowed up and spread like a dirty curtain over the houses. Minutes before and the men would have been buried under the rubble.

Climbing out of the ditches where they had taken shelter, they patted the dust from their uniforms and hurried to the safety of the wood. Ernie had been born and bred in the countryside and knew how to read the signs that nature left as warnings. Not a bird was singing. Rabbits scuttled for cover.

He loved the countryside but he also loved the army. He was young and healthy and had joined as a boy soldier at 16. As well as learning infantry drill, he had been trained to play the drums in the Regimental band. Dressed in the ceremonial dress of leopard-skin and watching the men keep step to the beats of his drum filled him with enormous pride.

He was proud too that from his princely wages of 10 shillings per week he could send money home to his mother. Even prouder that he was highly regarded as an expert marksman with both rifle and **Bren** gun. It came naturally to him. He and his brother had hunted rabbits as soon as they were old enough to hold a gun.

Once under cover of the woods the soldiers settled down to brewing tea, smoking cigarettes, thinking of home and wondering what was in store for them. What would their orders be? Would they be in the thick of the fighting?

Ernie leaned against the thick trunk of an oak tree and looked up at the dappled sunlight through the canopy of trees. He was anxious. What he feared most of all was losing his nerve. Shaming himself in front of his mates. He felt he would not let anyone down but there was one thing that made him squirm more than anything else.

Bayonets! He winced at the thought. They'd been taught how to use one. It all sounded so mechanical. 'Push it in, twist it and then rip it out.' And they'd practised on stuffed dummies, screaming at the straw effigies in order to screw up their courage. But the thought of doing it to another human being or, worse still, have the enemy do it to you, made his blood run cold.

The Plan

Daylight faded into night. Captain Barclay and some of

the sergeants told the men to gather round. In the pale light of hurricane lamps, the officers began to explain what they were to do.

Captain Barclay cleared his throat. 'The Germans are pouring over the frontier. Our duty is to stop them. We will be crossing into Belgium, which is under attack. There we will pick up our motor transport and head for the front.

'Now, men, it only remains for me to tell you that our "holiday" is over. Now, more than ever, your training will stand you in good stead. Keep your heads down and your spirits high, and from now on when you aim your rifle to shoot, you shoot to kill.'

Forming up in silent columns, they set off in the evening gloom, approaching the Belgian frontier by small back roads. They reached their lorries without incident and headed in the direction of the enemy. Progress was slow, for the roads were flooded with refugees. Bicycles, old prams, any wheeled transport that would carry their meagre possessions, filled the roads to bursting point. Heads were bent in dejection; children's faces stained with tears.

Stuka Attack

Stranded in the slow-moving streams of desperate civilians, the soldiers became easy targets for the Stuka dive-bombers. The German pilots dived from towering heights, spraying machine-gun bullets and dropping bombs into the midst of the terrified groups of people.

Bundles of clothing were left scattered on the roadside as the refugees ran for cover.

Ernie and the others tumbled out of the back of the lorries and rolled into the ditches. The Stuka bombers were terrifying. Sirens were fitted to their wheels and there were whistles on the bombs so that they sounded like a tribe of monstrous banshees raging in the skies. Ernie shook like a jelly.

Company Sergeant Major Gristock ordered the men to pull themselves together and to 'get fell in'. But when he thought they weren't looking, he cast an anxious eye towards the skies. 'Where are the "boys in blue" when you most need them?' he thought to himself. They hadn't seen any sign of the RAF all day.

In Full Retreat

The onslaught of the German advance could not be halted and the BEF found itself fighting rearguard actions as it retreated through Belgium and back into France. Grim evidence of their defeat was everywhere. Bodies lay by the roadside. Burnt-out shells of lorries and motorcycles lay like charred skeletons across the road. Abandoned artillery guns pointed forlornly to the sky. And everywhere there were signs of panic as soldiers had dropped their equipment to ease their escape. Terrified refugees streamed through the litter of defeat, making troop movement almost impossible.

But discipline had remained tight in Ernie Leggett's

battalion during their four-day retreat. Orders arrived for them to form a defensive line along the river Escaut, where a German attack was expected any hour. Taking cover in a cement factory, Ernie and his comrades could look out to woods on the opposite bank from the balconies that jutted out from the building. Even though there was no sign of movement, they knew the Germans must be over there. Dragging tables and boxes to the balconies, the soldiers barricaded the windows and doors and set up their Bren guns to give a broad sweep of the woods and far embankment. Ammunition was stacked and ready and sentries were posted. Ernie wrapped himself in his army blanket and tried to get some sleep. Despite the hard floor, he was soon fast asleep, exhausted by the days spent in retreat.

Under Attack

The sunlight streamed in through the windows and woke Ernie from his deep sleep. He rubbed his eyes and joined the corporal who was peering at the woods opposite. An eerie silence hung over the woods. No birds sang and even the river seemed uncannily still. A low moaning wind swept through the long grass.

As Ernie and the corporal scanned the far bank for signs of the enemy, they spotted several German officers talking and pointing to the factory. Seconds later, squads of soldiers appeared at the edge of the woods, hauling boats down to the water.

A rush of excitement coursed through Ernie's body.

The moment of truth had finally arrived. Ernie raised his rifle and took aim.

The corporal raised his arm and placed it on the barrel of Ernie's rifle. 'No, not yet. Captain Barclay will give the signal. We'll catch them on the move.'

The Germans clambered down the bank. They must have known that the British were on the opposite bank but this did not deter them from carrying out their orders.

Captain Barclay was fearless and had an odd way of showing it. He carried a hunting horn wherever he went, which he used to signal orders to his men. Captain Barclay placed it to his lips and sounded the attack. A volley of rifle fire crashed from the British line. German soldiers dropped where they stood or scattered for the limited cover that lined the river bank.

Ernie took careful aim. His chosen target, a German crawling down to the canal. Ernie squeezed the trigger gently, the man jerked suddenly and then stopped moving.

The corporal turned to Ernie and gave him an approving smile. 'Here! Take this for a while.'

The corporal handed the stock of the section Bren gun to Ernie who fitted it into the crook of his shoulder. Before he could fire, Private May, lying on the other side of Ernie, gave a grunt and fell forward. A small trickle of blood ran down his forehead from an ugly hole in his temple.

Ernie whispered the Lord's Prayer as the Bren gun

stuttered into action. Machine-guns and mortars opened up from the opposite bank. Half-track vehicles crashed through the undergrowth and perched on the embankment, opening up a steady fire on the cement factory.

'Thy will be done . . .' Ernie continued to mouth the prayer, summoning courage from the repetition of the familiar words. Bullets were flying everywhere. The Bren gun juddered as it spat bullets out at the German soldiers still making their way down to the canal and it took Ernie all his strength to aim it accurately. By this time all the men were shouting out their own prayers and oaths – most of it sheer nonsense.

Spent shell cases clinked across the concrete floor as Ernie fired the gun in short bursts. German soldiers spun backward from the impact of his bullets or juddered as they fell into the long grass and bushes of the river bank.

There was very little cover for the German attackers and panic was beginning to set in. At last they broke and retreated to the cover of the woods.

'Cease fire!' Captain Barclay's orders boomed out and the rifle fire fell silent. Once again the low moan of the wind could be heard through the long grass. In the moment's silence that followed, it dawned on Ernie and his comrades that they had defeated the enemy attack. A muffled cheer rang out, echoing around the blood-stained walls and floor.

By mid-afternoon on 21 May the Germans had pin-pointed the positions of the British soldiers and were picking them off with sniper fire. Two had already been killed and one was carried downstairs screaming. Ernie had tried to block out the sound.

The situation was steadily getting worse. The corporal had been killed, picked out by a sniper as he tried to remove the over-heated barrel of the Bren gun. Worst of all, the mortars were slowly but inevitably blasting the walls of the factory to pieces. The section was now down to four men but those that remained hung on to their positions grimly.

Ernie peered out of the balcony and saw an English soldier crawling towards the river over open ground. He was working his way closer and closer to a machine-gun nest. What the soldier did not realize and could not see was that the Germans were setting up a second machine-gun position close by.

Springing up from the long grass, the English soldier lobbed a grenade at the first machine-gunners, shooting them with his rifle as they scattered for cover. But he was now in full view of the other machine-gun and stood no chance. The second machine-gunners swung round their weapon and in a swift burst of gunfire cut the man down. Ernie could not see who it was but learned later that it was their own Company Sergeant Major George Gristock. The CSM died of his wounds and was later awarded the Victoria Cross for his bravery on that day.

Ernie had little time to take in what he had seen before a mortar bomb crashed in through the smashed roof. Ernie was sent spinning through the air, hitting the ceiling and landing with a dull thud. A pool of blood slowly spread out from beneath his body.

Two of Ernie's comrades raced to his side. Ripping the trousers from his legs, they exposed a savage wound in Ernie's groin. If it had severed his main artery he was finished. He would be dead within a minute. But Ernie's mates were not going to give up on him. Plugging the huge hole with field dressings, they tied the whole bundle together with a tourniquet. Ernie was carried downstairs and gently placed in an outhouse where they left him. He was unaware of all of this for he had fallen unconscious. When he woke up, he knew that he must make it back to their headquarters, otherwise he might well die or get left behind.

He struggled to his feet and immediately fell over. He would have to crawl. A railway line at the back of the factory offered meagre cover but it was all there was. He dragged his half-naked body along. A trail of blood marked his route. He lost consciousness once more.

I must have passed out because the next thing I felt was my wrists being pulled. And I looked up into the faces of two men who I knew well. They were both clarinet players in the band. And they said 'It's Ernie.'

And as I faded into unconsciousness again I heard one say to the other, 'He's had it.'

But Ernie had not 'had it'. Bundled aboard a 15-hundred weight truck he was bumped, jostled and jolted all the way back to Dunkirk. The doctors had injected him with morphine to deaden the pain. Ernie was confused during this time. At times he thought he was still travelling to the front to fight Germans, at others walking around St Peter's Church in his own village of Clippersby. Evacuated from Dunkirk on a hospital ship, he eventually arrived back in Blighty. Only then did he feel safe and rested and could confidently say, 'Thank God I'm home.'

Ernie is still living, although the wound that he received that day still twinges and aches. And every Remembrance Day, Ernie plays the bugle in honour of all those not as fortunate as himself who did not make it home but lie in a grave in France.

1939 – The 'Phoney' War

Unbelievably, the British and French did little to come to the aid of Poland, preferring to wait for the Germans to attack them. For nearly eight months they simply stood and stared at one another.

The Germans cynically called this period of the war *sitzkrieg* or 'sitting war' – so unlike the *blitzkrieg*, or 'lightning war', that they had unleashed against Poland and were soon to unleash on France.

FIGHTING FACTS

Tanks 1940

	Max. Speed (mph)	Weight (tons)	Number available	Number in crew
France				
Somua S35	25	20	260	3
Renault R35	12.5	9.8	950	2
Char BI	17.5	32	311	4
Hotchkiss H35	17.5	11.5	545	2
Hotchkiss H39	22.5	12	276	2
Britain				
Matilda MkII	15	26.5	75	4
A10	18	14	126	5
A13	30	14	30	4
Germany				
PzKwII	16	9	1095	3
PzKwIII	25	19.3	388	5
PzKw 38(t)	26	9.7	410	4
PzKw 35(t)	25	10.5	273	4
PzKwIV	18.5	17.3	278	5

Gordon Waterfield, British war correspondent for a daily newspaper, was disgusted by the attitude of the British army:

Across the river a young German was standing in the sun, naked to the waist, washing himself. It annoyed me that it should be possible for him to go on washing calmly there with two machine-guns facing him on the opposite bank. I asked the sentry why he did not fire. He seemed surprised at my bloodthirstiness and said, 'We are not wicked and besides, if we fire they will only fire back at us.'

Blitzkrieg Terror

The Germans had perfected a new kind of warfare called *blitzkrieg*. Air attacks were blended with massed tank units and motorized infantry. This meant that the Germany army could punch holes in the enemy's defences and move in fast to surround them. During the battle for France some of the tank units covered as much as 40–60 miles a day. Curiously, both British and French military writers had recommended *blitzkrieg* tactics but only the Germans had put them into practice.

Exhaustion

During the retreat to Dunkirk few soldiers had time to rest, let alone sleep, but the 1st East Surrey battalion finally invented a way to doze a little on the march. By linking arms, two outside men could walk a man between them as he slept. From time to time they'd switch places with one another.

Belgium's Surrender

The Germans quickly overran Belgium. When the Belgians surrendered they left a huge gap in the British and French armies, which had to be quickly plugged.

One Belgian officer refused to obey the order and set off for the French lines. Staying in the war was not as easy as he thought, however. A French sentry accused him of being a traitor and a coward and warned that he would shoot him if he came any closer. Turned back, he made his way to the British lines. They were afraid that he might be a spy and refused to let him through. Eventually, joining up with other Belgians he boarded a fishing boat and made for England.

Saved by the Panzers

The Germans too were exhausted by the speed of their advance and stopped to rest on Hitler's orders, reassured by Goering that he could finish the British and French off with his **Luftwaffe**. Hitler ordered a further halt. This gave a valuable two days in which the British could arrange for the remnants of their army to escape from Dunkirk back to England.

Heinz Guderian, commander of the Panzer Tank army, was amazed at the decision. 'We were utterly speechless. Just over the horizon lay Dunkirk. The BEF could have been destroyed on the beaches.'

Dunkirk – Defeat or Victory?

Between 24 May and 3 June 1941 over 200,000 British and over 100,000 French soldiers were evacuated to Britain, leaving the Allies with an army to continue the fight against Nazi Germany.

British troops on the beaches of Dunkirk, under attack
from the German Luftwaffe.

The Grim Reality

British Expeditionary Casualties	68,111 killed, wounded or taken prisoner
Equipment abandoned	Artillery guns 2,472 Rifles 90,000 Vehicles 63,879 Motorcycles 20,548 Stores and Ammunition 500,000 tons
Ships Sunk at Dunkirk	243 out of 860
Aircraft Lost	474

A painting of the scene
at Dunkirk.

The Hope

Troops evacuated
338,226 (139,097 French)
These remained the only
trained troops left to defend
Britain but they were without most of their equipment.

What Saved the British?

The weather. The English Channel rarely stays calm but
for nine days during the evacuation of Dunkirk the sea
remained like a millpond.

• Overhead mists and rain seemed to come at the right
moment. The Luftwaffe mounted three assaults on

Dunkirk and each time low cloud prevented a follow-up.

• Hitler's order of 24 May, halting his tanks just as they were closing in for the kill.

• Herman Goering announcing that the Luftwaffe alone could deal with the French and British armies.

• The determination of the British to rescue their army and the thousands of volunteers who brought their boats into the dangerous waters.

DESERT DUEL

BATTLE BRIEFING

Following the fall of France in May 1940, the Italian dictator Mussolini allied his country with Germany. This agreement between the dictators of Germany and Italy became the so-called 'Pact of Steel'. In reality, Italy was entirely dependent on its victorious neighbour north of the Alps.

This did not prevent Mussolini, however, from trying to prove that his country could be just as successful in military campaigns as Germany. Dreaming of the creation of a new Roman Empire in the Mediterranean, the Italian army invaded Greece, only to have the adventure end in embarrassing stalemate. Germany was forced to come to their rescue and conquer Greece.

In September 1941, Mussolini decided on another campaign. Crossing the frontier wire from their colony Cyrenaica, in North Africa, the Italians attacked the British in Egypt, at that time part of the British Empire. The small but well-trained British forces stopped them in their tracks and pushed them all the way back to Benghazi.

Again Germany was forced to bale out her ineffective ally. In 1941, Hitler especially chose one of his top generals, Erwin Rommel, to command this combined force of Italians and Germans (Axis powers) and strengthened their punch with three panzer (tank) divisions. This had an immediate and dramatic effect.

The Axis forces pushed the British back into Egypt and were soon poised to strike at Cairo and the Suez Canal. This would have secured the huge Middle Eastern oil reserves for Germany and cut Britain's link with India and her Empire in the Far East. The situation was perilous.

In July 1942, the Germans began to batter at the British defences at El Alamein, the last defensible line before Cairo. At this most dangerous moment the Germans were beaten back, suffering heavy losses.

The British now turned to the attack but each offensive quickly got bogged down. Both sides felt the stalemate couldn't continue and the British were desperate for a victory.

In defiant mood, but privately anxious, Winston Churchill, the British Prime Minister, visited Egypt on 5 August. He wished to encourage the troops by his presence but also to assess the situation for himself. Churchill decided a change at the top was necessary. General Auchinleck was relieved of his command and replaced by the somewhat eccentric General Bernard Montgomery.

Montgomery was a perfectionist in his military duties but a rather lonely and arrogant commander. Many soldiers of the Eighth Army, however, saw his arrogance as a sign that he had confidence in his ability to win battles, and he soon inspired considerable trust. He toured all the divisions within his army and gave simple but inspiring speeches to the men, often from the bonnet of his jeep.

He would not go into battle until he was absolutely ready. Churchill kept demanding action but Montgomery insisted that victory would not happen until he had built up sufficient resources and his battle plan had been perfected.

Throughout September 1942 the Germans attempted to break through the British defensive lines but they held fast. On 23 September, Rommel fell ill and was flown home on sick leave. This misfortune for the Axis forces was to assist the British.

On 23 October 1942, Montgomery launched his long-anticipated attack. Bill Norris was a commander of one of his tanks.

Date: 23 October– 4 November 1942
Place: The Western Desert, Egypt

Tank Command

Bill Norris sank back into the luxury of a bath brimming with hot, soapy water. It had been a long time since he felt he could relax. After being chased by Rommel's forces thousands of miles across the desert and eating when and what he could, Bill was enjoying this moment

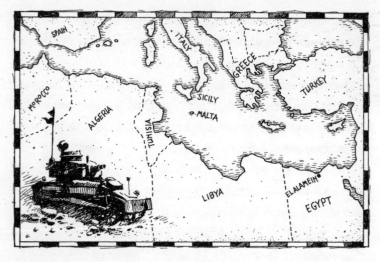

North Africa.

away from the battlefield. They'd all taken a real mauling and were in a sorry state. The order had then gone out to prepare a defensive line at El Alamein – less than a day's march from the Suez Canal. If the German tanks made a breakthrough they would be finished. 'Still,' Bill thought to himself, 'we've got a new commander. Spindly blighter, this Monty chap, but very sure of himself.'

But for a few brief moments he could forget all these things for there were more treats in store – real food and a real bed! Bill smiled to himself. It wasn't just the luxuries he was now enjoying that pleased him but the reason he'd been sent to Alexandria in the first place. 'At last,' he thought, 'we have a tank which will settle the enemy. We've been out-gunned by the Germans for too long. It's true they're tough, not like the Italians, but they're not unbeatable. And now we've got the tank that's going to even things up!'

Bill had been sent to the port of Alexandria in Egypt to take delivery of eighteen gleaming monsters. The Sherman tank, manufactured in America, was a good match for the German tanks. It was thirty tons of 3-inch armour plating, bristling with a magnificent 75 mm turret gun and three machine-guns and could roar into battle at 25 mph. He couldn't wait to see the men's faces when they saw their new weapon.

Jumping Off

'Tomorrow . . . tomorrow's the day.' The order for the next day flashed around the Eight Army like a terrible secret that needed to be whispered. But there was little time for the men to dwell on their personal thoughts for much had to be done. Ammunition, rations and fuel had to be checked and loaded aboard. Crews had to become familiar with their new Sherman tanks.

By early evening all was ready. At 21:40 precisely on 23 October, a furious Allied barrage of 882 guns lit the night sky with so many rounds fired that it seemed as if daylight had come early that morning. The ground trembled and the air vibrated. Bombers droned overhead and the bombs crashed like thunder. Four infantry divisions with fixed bayonets advanced. Moonlight glinted on their weapons.

The order was given for Bill's tanks to move to their

An artillery barrage lights the night sky.

jumping-off position in front of the minefields, which they reached the following day. And there, in the shimmering heat of the desert, was their objective. There were very few recognizable locations in the desert, but opposite them was a crumbling ridge, casting a dark shadow over the surrounding wasteland. This was their target.

Smoky dusk settled over the desert and then vanished into the blue-blackness of night. Bill and his crew were waiting for the order to advance once a path through the minefields had been cleared. He admired the men who did this, who risked death and terrible injury every day. It was their job to find the mines and dig them up. Every metre of terrain had to be cleared by gingerly prodding the sand with a bayonet, for only a few of them had mine-detectors and they weren't always very effective. The steel had to be kept at about a thirty-degree angle – any steeper and the mine could detonate. Some mines were booby-trapped and the slightest pressure on their surface would detonate them. Often trip wires linked several mines together and when one was removed it detonated the others, usually with fatal consequences but sometimes leaving a crippling injury to arm, foot or leg.

In this rare moment of calm before a battle, Bill surveyed his crew. His wireless operator had died during the last battle with the Germans. He'd been sitting alongside Bill on the turret of the tank when a red-hot shell splinter pierced his upper arm and lanced straight into his heart. It was almost impossible to use the periscope accurately and at least one man, the commander or one of his crew, usually had his head protruding from the top, directing the fight. This made him a sitting target.

Bill's new wireless operator was a ladies' hairdresser from London and the crew boasted the best haircuts in the regiment. He was also a superlative cook and a genius at transforming bully beef and hard biscuits into meals that at least looked edible.

Bill's gunner was an Irishman. The driver was a giant

blond Norwegian, who'd escaped from his country after the Germans had invaded. Because of his massive height he was nicknamed 'Tiny'. And what strength! He once broke a track on a tank by heaving at the steering wheel too hard. The second driver was Jewish. He never got into a 'spin' in battle but calmly worked away at firing the machine-gun. They were good people to have around. Despite being from so many different backgrounds, they were bound together in their hatred of the Nazis.

Into the Storm of Battle

By the evening of the 24th a ten-mile path had been cleared through the minefield and Bill's tank crew could advance on the enemy. Light reconnaissance Crusader tanks led the way, followed by heavier Grants and finally Bill's beloved Shermans. Two searchlight beams lit either side of the track to prevent the Allied tanks straying into uncleared minefields.

Bill looked up into the heavens. The stars appeared no more than tiny, twinkling dots of light. The moon was bright and silvered the tanks as they crawled at a snail's pace towards the enemy lines. Fortunately, there was no wind but the thousands of vehicles on the move churned up so much dust that the drivers were unable to see ahead and relied on instructions from the commanders sitting above the turrets of the tanks.

Ahead of Bill and the tanks the Allied bomber planes were at work. Flashes streaked the sky, whilst red mushroom clouds of flames billowed into the night when a fuel or ammunition dump was hit.

Suddenly, by some strange coincidence all the engines stalled, except for one lone Crusader which ploughed on, perilously alone. It then pulled up and towed a tank behind it, managing to get it started again. One by one the tanks gradually re-started. Bill cursed. For a moment they had been sitting targets. Fortunately the Germans had not responded.

As dawn silvered the horizon, they were clear of the minefields and heading down a long reverse slope towards their objective at the top of the ridge. As they climbed the track, they passed the burnt-out shells of a regiment of Shermans, all knocked out by anti-tank guns. They'd been caught as they were silhouetted on top of the ridge by the setting sun the previous night.

Enemy locations were spotted up ahead and the tank commanders took sightings through their binoculars and directed the fire. Some German shells caused a few casualties but after the pounding they received from the Allies, they began to withdraw to second line defences.

As Bill began to appreciate the pause in the battle, a tank to his left suddenly exploded, the turret shooting twenty feet into the air. At first, it was thought that a stray shell from the fleeing enemy had hit it until the blackened faces of the tank crew crawled from the wreckage.

'Stupid stoves,' they mouthed in exasperation. Bill's

crew smiled, knowing too well the dangers of the little petrol stoves they were equipped with to make a 'brew-up' for tea. They'd blown themselves up!

As they waited for their orders, a group of about 100 German prisoners, fingers laced together and held on top of their heads, filed past the tanks. They got no further. A gunner in one of the Shermans opened fire at them and the prisoners crumpled, screaming, before dying of their wounds. Before the gunner could extend his field of fire, the machine-gun was wrestled from his hands and he was dragged from the vehicle. Bill learned later that the gunner's brother had been killed in a previous engagement and the soldier could think of nothing but revenge. He was taken into custody and Bill never saw him again.

That night the tanks were corralled in a circle like a wagon train expecting an Indian attack. The infantry dug in around the perimeter. This was the most dangerous of times, for enemy infantry often filtered through tank lines and opened fire.

Turning the Tide of War

The battle boiled on for several days. The men could scarcely keep awake and snatched what little sleep they could. Bill and his men were at the centre of the battle-field but most of the action was taking place to the north where, after heavy losses, the Allies began to force the Germans into retreat. Rommel, who had returned to the front, although still ill, gave orders for a withdrawal.

Now was the moment to throw the enemy off

balance. Bill and his fellow tank commanders raced in a north-westerly direction to begin to surround and cut off the enemy. But they were too late, for Rommel and the Afrika Corps were already beginning to flee back along the coast road, abandoning masses of equipment in their hurried retreat.

And then, as if the Germans had won an ally in the weather, the rains came on 1 November. Any thought of rapid pursuit became bogged down in the winter rains.

Bill surveyed the wreckage of battle. As the rain pattered down upon the desert sands, tiny flowers began to bloom in their millions. And with the rains, the victory at El Alamein turned the tide of war when Montgomery launched Operation Supercharge on 2 November, which began to outflank the Axis forces. In Britain, church bells,

Wounded British soldiers await an
Advanced Dressing Station.

which had remained silent and were only to be rung if a German invasion took place, pealed out in victory.

The fighting was far from over but, as Churchill said, El Alamein was, 'Not the end, not even the beginning of the end but the end of the beginning of the war.' Before, Bill had hoped for victory – El Alamein proved it was possible. Rommel, despite his reputation, could be outfought. Britain now had a general who rivalled that of the Germans.

FIGHTING FACTS

Naming the Battle

El Alamein took its name from a lonely railway station just over a mile from the coast. The Allied defensive line stretched from this railway station some 40 miles to the south where it ended at the Quatra Depression, a huge range of hills surrounding a vast bowl of treacherous sand. No vehicle could travel through this southerly area so there was no danger that the Germans could circle behind the Eighth Army.

The Duelists

Bernard Law Montgomery was born the son of a bishop in 1887 and spent his youth in Tasmania, Australia, before his family moved to England. Not a very popular student at Sandhurst, the military college for officers, he made his mark through hard work. On the Western Front in World War I he won the Distinguished Service Order for bravery.

Montgomery had the reputation of being an eccentric, although he was a perfectionist when carrying out his military duties. Despite writing a book on infantry tactics, his promotion was slow before the war. His appointment as a commander of the battered Eighth Army in August 1942 was to prove a turning point in his career, however, and in the British army's campaign. His victory over the Axis forces made him a hero and he was honoured with the title of Viscount Montgomery of Alamein, although his men affectionately called him Monty.

Erwin Rommel was born in 1891 the son of a school-teacher. In World War I he was so determined to win the Order of Merit he led his men into very ferocious fighting and he won the award.

After war ended he came to the attention of his army superiors as an inspiring teacher of tactics. His lectures were published in a book on infantry tactics. It was a best-seller and its fame brought him to the attention of Hitler. Rommel believed in Nazi ideals and lived only for his army career. When war broke out he was given command of a panzer division and played a major part in the fall of France.

Later, when the Italians were sent reeling in North

Africa by the Allies, Rommel was sent to stiffen resistance. He soon won new successes, driving the British forces back to Egypt. Fortunately for the Allies he became ill and was flown back to Germany whilst Montgomery built up his own forces for attack. Flying back to take command, Rommel fought a fierce battle at El Alamein but because his supply lines were so long he was forced to retreat. Nevertheless, he managed to withdraw his forces without capture.

Hitler, not wanting him to be tarnished with defeat, brought him back to Europe where he was put in charge of preparing the defences in France against an expected Allied invasion. After the Allies landed, Rommel became increasingly convinced that Germany would lose the war and was implicated in a plot against Hitler. As a Field-Marshall in the German army, Hitler did not want Rommel's disloyalty to be widely known so as a consequence he was given the option of committing suicide. Backed into a corner, Rommel chose to take his own life.

The Sherman Tank

The arrival of the American Sherman Tank in the deserts of North Africa came as a nasty shock to the German panzer crews. Bill collected one of the 252 tanks delivered to the Eighth Army in time for the battle of El Alamein. It was fast moving and had high firepower. Despite the brief breakdown of Bill's Sherman tanks at

El Alamein, it was magnificently reliable and mechanically efficient. By 1944, however, it was no match for the German Tiger and Panther tanks.

Facts about the Sherman

Weight	32 tons
Speed	24 mph
Armour	76 mm steel front
	56 mm steel side
Weapons	MkV 75 mm gun
	Penetration 74 mm of armour at 100 yards

Enemy Tanks

The Panzer IV was the most numerously produced German tank of the war. By 1944 it had passed its best but it was still a formidable opponent.

Facts about the Panzer Mark IV

Weight	25 tons
Speed	25 mph
Armour	80 mm front armour
	30 mm side armour
Weapons	75 mm gun could penetrate 99 mm of armour at 100 yards

---

Battle Strengths at El Alamein

	Axis Forces	Allied Forces
Aircraft	350	530
Tanks	489	1,029
Soldiers	104,000	195,000
Artillery	1,219	2,311

We Were Only Looking!

Two important Italian officers were captured by the Allies in the desert by a reconnaissance patrol. Brought back to headquarters for interrogation they complained bitterly that they had not taken part in any battle, they had only been observing British methods. The fact that they were enemies did not seem to strike either of them as strange and, as one of the angry pair announced, 'This is an absolute outrage. We were only looking!'

Desert Rats

It may seem strange for a soldier to want to be nick-named a 'rat', a name that conjures up dirt and filth or, when it's applied to a human being, someone who can't be trusted. But desert rats are a different type of rat altogether. They are clean, can bound along fast on long back legs and, above all, can live in the harsh conditions of the desert. For these reasons, soldiers of the Eighth Army were only too proud to be honoured by the nick-name of 'desert rats'.

RESISTANCE

BATTLE BRIEFING

People in countries occupied by the Germans had a difficult choice. They could try to get on with things as they were and work with the new government and armed forces, becoming collaborators. Or they could resist by passing on information about German troop movements or blowing up trains carrying enemy troops. To resist, of course, was highly dangerous.

A few brave men and women joined resistance groups but the German secret police were highly efficient and many resistors were killed or captured. No mercy was shown to prisoners, who were usually tortured before being executed.

Soon after the fall of France, resistance groups began to appear all over Europe but they were badly organized and were frequently destroyed. Britain quickly realized, however, the value of the military information these groups provided and began to parachute agents into occupied France.

Occupied Europe and North Africa.

These agents had to be alert at all times. Often tiny things betrayed them. One agent was arrested because he was looking for oncoming traffic in the direction he was used to in Britain.

From 1941 onwards the British and American Secret Services played an important role in organizing these secret armies, and women were in the forefront. They fought with machine-guns and grenades alongside their male comrades in the French Resistance.

*As the Germans began to lose the war more and more
people joined the Resistance movements. In remoter parts of
France, small armies called the Maquis were formed, which
did much to disrupt German troop movements when the
Allies landed on the Normandy coast. Pearl Witherington was
one of these brave fighters.*

Date: 23 September 1943
Place: RAF Tempsford airfield, Bedfordshire
Night Flight

Pearl Witherington studied the sky as the gloom gathered around the secret airfield at RAF Tempsford in
Bedfordshire. Hedged between the Great North road
and the main railway line from London to Edinburgh, few
flights took off from its concrete runways. For this reason, most passing visitors, as well as the locals themselves, dismissed this base as unimportant.

They were wrong to do so. In fact, Tempsford was one
of the main bases from which RAF Special Duties sent
secret agents into the heart of Nazi-occupied France.
The journey was perilous, and particularly so in the frag-
ile Lysanders and plodding Halifax aircraft. If they were
not caught in the searchlights and flak (anti-aircraft fire)
then the agents themselves could well be parachuting
into a trap set by the Germans, having been betrayed by
the people they had been sent to help.

Pearl understood the dangers only too well, for she
had already escaped from France once before. Trapped

in Paris by the unexpected speed of the German advance, Pearl and her parents and three sisters had no intention of 'sitting out' the war. As the German radio broadcast news of devastating bombing raids by the Luftwaffe on London in the autumn of 1940, the Witheringtons decided to make their bid for freedom.

To England

The first stage of their journey was to cross into the unoccupied area of France. The north and the Atlantic coastline were garrisoned by German troops. To the south and east, the French were allowed to set up a puppet government, answerable to their German masters. Marshall Petain, a World War I general, was brought out of retirement to head the collaborationist state of Vichy, named after the town which became its capital.

To cross the demarcation line was dangerous. Every French person had to carry a pass stamped by the Germans giving them permission to travel. All trains, cars and lorries were searched. Forging passes became a major industry from which fortunes could be made. It was a perilous trade. If caught, the guilty could expect long prison sentences.

Pearl, a secretary in the British embassy, managed to get papers and tickets to Marseilles in the unoccupied zone of France but it took just about all her family's savings. Arriving hungry and penniless in Marseilles, they hoped to get passage aboard a Red Cross ship back to England but the ship never came. Meanwhile, Pearl kept her family in whatever food was available. Horsemeat and lungs were frequently on the menu, being the cheapest cuts of meat.

Crossing the Pyrenees

Pearl was not the sort of woman to sit and wait for things to happen. She persuaded the rest of the family that as the Red Cross ship was unlikely to arrive, their only alternative was to cross the Pyrenees into neutral Spain. They made their way to Gibraltar, a British colony, and found room on a troopship returning from Egypt.

On 14 July 1941 they sailed into Glasgow. Determined to enlist in the forces as soon as they landed, Pearl's two younger sisters, Mimi and Jackie, immediately joined the WAAF (Women's Auxiliary Air Force). But before their training could begin, the newspapers got hold of their story. They became immediate celebrities, having run great risks to get back to England to serve their country. 'They Walked a Thousand Miles to join the WAAF' trumpeted the headlines.

Pearl was pleased but was content to remain in the background and obtained a humdrum job at the Air Ministry. But after the excitement of their daring escape, Pearl soon grew bored with the routine work of a secretary. Hearing vague rumours about secret operations in France, Pearl went to her boss and volunteered. Such work was 'hush-hush', however, and Peal was refused permission. Secret Operations preferred to make their own approach and sometimes in odd ways.

Undeterred, Pearl made further inquiries and learned that there was an office at 82 Baker Street that had something to do with the Secret Operations group. As a secret organization it was careful not to advertise its presence. Situated down a narrow alley, the door plaque simply stated, 'Inter-Services Research Bureau'.

Volunteer for Danger

Pearl braced herself and marched in. On the top floor, a tall man with thinning hair offered her a seat and let her speak without interruption. Pearl did not know it at the time but this was no other than Colonel Maurice Buckmaster, head of Special Operations Executive, F section (F for French).

Pearl spoke with passion of her hatred of the Nazi conquerors and she did so in fluent French. When she had finished, Buckmaster held out his hand. 'Thank you, Miss Witherington. This has been a most interesting interview. I will be in touch.'

Several weeks later, as Pearl began to think she'd been forgotten, she received a call. She was to report to Wanborough Manor, where she was put through a tough mental and physical training programme. Agents were not released into France unless their trainers were convinced they would survive. They had to live, breathe, eat and think as French people. Woken up in the middle of the night, they had to remember to reply in French and not English.

After five months of gruelling training Pearl was ready

to return to France. She could say nothing to her family about her destination and they simply had to accept that she had gone missing 'on duty'.

To France

The Halifax bomber was waiting for her, purring on the runway. She checked her equipment and heard a 'good luck' coming from the shadows as her trainer wished her well. She turned and climbed into the small Hillman truck that would take her across the airfield to the looming shadow of her transport aircraft. She felt the night close in around her. She was alone, utterly alone and there was no turning back.

There were no comforts in the Halifax bomber. It was not designed with that in mind. Pearl tried to settle down for the journey ahead into occupied Europe but the noisy aircraft constantly vibrated, and it was freezing cold. The engine roared as it tried to pick up enough revs for take-off. At 125 miles per hour, the aircraft lurched into the air, as Pearl's stomach flipped over.

Pearl had been given an important mission. She was to be second in command to Squadron Leader Maurice Southgate who had been entrusted with a vast area of France stretching from the Loire to the Pyrenees. A number of armed Maquis resistance fighters were operating in this area and their underground war against the Germans needed coordinating. Pearl and Maurice already knew one another from when they had both been employed in the Air Ministry. It was an ideal partnership, for they both liked and respected one another. Pearl was not to know, however, that Maurice had a special assignment in mind for her.

The shuddering bomber flew low over France, picking its route carefully to avoid main towns where it would attract anti-aircraft fire. The navigator checked his calculations by glancing through the aircraft windows, looking for recognizable rivers glinting in the moonlight and the dark shadows of hill ranges and mountains.

Pearl heard the shuffling creak of a leather flying jacket as one of the aircrew made his way along the fuselage towards her. 'Miss Witherington, soon be over the drop zone. We've got you safely there. Just came to check your gear,' he said cheerfully, hoping that his good spirits would fill Pearl with confidence. He pulled at her webbing and harness, making sure it was secure, before clipping her to the static line that stretched the length of the fuselage. This would automatically open Pearl's parachute as soon as she jumped.

He tapped her on the shoulder, a beaming smile on his lips as he gave her a reassuring thumbs-up. Turning his back to her, he wrestled the exit door open. A blast of cold air rushed into the cabin and Pearl stared out into the star-pricked sky.

A red light flashed above the door, flickered for a few moments, then turned to green.

'Go!' snapped the RAF officer.

Pearl jumped before she had time to think about what she was doing. She hurtled away from the Halifax and safety into the silent night sky. The parachute flapped open and soon she was sailing down towards blotches of trees and open fields.

As she raced towards the ground, shadows ran from clumps of bushes towards her. Could they be German? She peered into the dark, trying to distinguish whether the figures were wearing steel helmets. As she thumped to the ground the figures reached out for her, pulling the silk of the parachute to one side.

'Pearl . . . Pearl, it's me Maurice.' Maurice's strong embrace raised her to her feet. 'Come on! We can't hang around here.'

The Reunion

Maurice bundled her into a car and, taking little back roads, they arrived at a farmhouse in the next district. As the door opened, the warm light that bathed the parlour dazzled Pearl. She blinked. She could scarcely believe what she saw. A man strode towards her, his face split by a broad smile and his arms held wide to hug her.

'Henri . . . Henri Cornioley! How can it be? You were taken by the Germans.' Pearl was puzzled but delighted that her childhood friend was free and there in the room.

'Pearl. How have you been? What's a nice girl like you doing mixing with dangerous people like us?' he joked.

Henri explained what had happened to him since they

had last met. After escaping from a German prisoner of war camp, he'd joined the French Resistance. Now they were to work together.

The Maquis

Pearl's first task was a difficult one. The French colonel who commanded the local Maquis group was a stubborn individual. His men were in desperate need of reorganization and re-equipping but he wanted things to stay as they always had been. Pearl went to work on him with all her charm. One hour later he was agreeing with her, two hours later and he was giving orders in line with Pearl's wishes.

Pearl worked tirelessly throughout the winter months of 1943 giving recruits weapon-training, planting explosives on railway lines and organizing receptions in drop zones.

All agents had to be suspicious of anyone and everyone. They could not afford to relax for a moment and this put a tremendous strain on them. It took only a brief lapse of concentration and an agent could fall into the hands of the Gestapo – the German secret police. On 1 May disaster struck.

Maurice made his fatal mistake on that hot day. Maybe he was tired from the heat or constantly being on his guard. Whatever the reason, his mistake was costly. Dashing to the house of a wireless operator in Paris, he forgot to check whether the 'all clear' signal was in place – a towel hanging from the windowsill. Maurice burst into the room and straight into the arms of the Gestapo. Punched and jostled, he was handcuffed and marched off to their headquarters. But despite rough treatment, torture and imprisonment he survived.

Pearl was left in sole command of Maurice's operations and at a particularly crucial time. The Germans knew by the increased bombardment of railway lines and by wireless messages that an Allied invasion was about to take place, but they were not sure where it would be. As a precaution, they began to step up their raids on suspicious houses.

Pearl narrowly escaped arrest herself when she was bounding up the stairs to a contact's house. She'd reached the first landing when a loud hiss stopped her in her tracks. 'Come down,' the caretaker of the building mouthed to her. 'The Gestapo are waiting for you.'

Night after night, Pearl ordered her 3,000 Maquis fighters into action. The main Paris railway line was cut several times. Telephone and telegraph wires were blown up or cut. Soon the Germans put a price on her head, offering one million francs for her capture. Posters showing her picture and detailing the reward were plastered all over the region.

On 5 June, the Maquis began to fight German troops in the open, drawing their soldiers away from Normandy, where the Allies were to land. Many Frenchmen were killed in these skirmishes. On one occasion, 11 June,

Pearl and 150 French resistance fighters were surrounded by 2,500 German soldiers. At one point in the
fire fight, Pearl was trapped in a cornfield. The Germans
sprayed their bullets everywhere but, miraculously, Pearl
wriggled on her belly out of danger. As she recalled:

> I had to be very careful how I moved. I watched the
> heads of the corn above me and as the breeze stirred
> them I moved a little closer to the edge of the field. I
> had to wait until the wind moved the corn, otherwise
> the Boche would have noticed it moving and fired
> directly at that spot. But they finally gave up and I
> managed to get away.

Honouring a Hero

In the middle of September 1944 Pearl's region of
France had been liberated and she handed over command of her Resistance group to a French officer. Her
force had been responsible for the deaths of 1,000
German soldiers and the capture of a further 20,000.

When she returned to England it would have been
expected that she should have received the highest honour in the land. Indeed, she was recommended for the
Military Cross but objections were raised because this
honour was for men not for women. In a 'man's world',
no one could imagine that a woman could have such
startling bravery. Instead, Pearl was sent the MBE (Medal
of the British Empire) Civil, which was a medal given to
civilians for acts of bravery. Pearl sent it back. A few

weeks later, she was offered another MBE but this time in recognition of her military exploits.

This, however, is not quite the end of the story. Shortly before the war ended, Pearl married her childhood sweetheart, Henri Cornioley and went to live in Paris, in the country which they had done much to help liberate.

FIGHTING FACTS

The Results of Resistance

Intelligence information

By the end of the war Allied intelligence information was excellent. It came from a number of sources.

Resistance groups throughout Europe had painstakingly built up networks of contacts, which gave information about German troop positions and movements.

Early in the war British agents captured a German coding machine, called an Enigma, from a German U-boat. The Germans thought their codes were unbreakable but they were wrong. As a result masses of battle orders became known to the Allies throughout the war. This information was distributed to the Allied commanders and leaders under the code name 'Ultra'. The British wished to keep their source of information secret so that the Germans would not change their coding machines. Some 'Ultra' information was of very high quality, including some of Hitler's operational orders.

An Enigma code machine.

Deception

The Allies' attempts to fool the Germans had some notable successes. In one instance an actor played the part of General Montgomery, and once a dead body was dumped in the Mediterranean Sea with false plans for the invasion of Europe in his pockets. 'Fortitude', the plan to disguise Allied landings in Normandy, achieved 100 per cent success.

Other deceptions included reports that General Patton, a famous American general, was touring a mythical invasion army in England. And plans for an invasion of Norway kept German forces scattered all over Europe. Even when the Allies finally landed in Normandy, Hitler refused to give orders for reserves to be committed to the battle, as he believed the landings themselves were a deception.

Escape

The British helped to set up escape lines, particularly to bring back aircrews who had been shot down. By 1944, for every airman captured an equal number was assisted back home. At that time it cost up to £15,000 to train a single fighter pilot and £23,000 to train the seven-man crew of a Lancaster bomber. In today's figures, the cost of training a fighter pilot would be approximately £500,000. Britain needed those men!

In all, 33,517 people in the armed forces returned from enemy-held territory during the war. Out of these 23,208 escaped. Most of these escapees were aircrew.

Sabotage

Factory sabotage in occupied countries made a large dent in the German war effort. Agents in France carried out about 150 attacks on French factories, mines and power installations. In few cases did they bring production to a full stop, however. Probably the most important raid by resistance fighters was in Rjukan, in Norway, when a German plant making materials for an atomic bomb was effectively knocked out.

Results of sabotage on a train carrying
German troops, 30 July 1943.

Attacks on troops

Isolated attacks often brought savage reprisals from the
German and Italian armies. When Heydrich, the commander of German intelligence in Czechoslovakia, was
assassinated, orders were given for all the inhabitants of
the village of Lidice to be massacred. In France a similar
massacre occurred at Oradour sur Glane.

However, there is no doubt that the **partisans** in
Russia kept many German soldiers on occupation
duties, and the rising of the French resistance fighters –
the Maquis – in France kept German divisions busy.

The Stress of Being an Agent

Secret agents were under enormous pressure not to

Book with a hiding place for a pistol.

betray themselves or their comrades. The slightest drop in their guard could give them away. Surprisingly, when Maurice Southgate was arrested he remembers a sense of relief, thinking, 'At last I can sleep.'

Plastic Explosives
In 1943 a new weapon was dropped to resistance groups. Plastic explosive was safe to carry around and could produce the same destructive results as several heavy bombers. This meant they could be even more effective in their sabotage of German troops.

Charles de Gaulle
Charles de Gaulle, a French army officer, set up the Free

French Forces in 1940 in order to continue fighting against Germany. They fought with the Allies in Africa, Italy and France. By 1944 there were more than 300,000 regular troops, and the Resistance had acknowledged de Gaulle's leadership. De Gaulle became a national hero, and the symbol for a free France, after entering Paris in triumph on 26 August 1944.

Collaborators

In Norway the Germans put a collaborator called Quisling in power. He tried to change school history books in line with Nazi ideas. Every history teacher in Norway refused to teach from the new books and was arrested. Eventually, because the prisons became so crowded they had to be released.

The Plot to Kill Hitler

Resistance in Germany was even more dangerous. In 1944 a plot to kill Hitler nearly succeeded. Lieutenant Colonel Count von Stauffenberg planted a bomb under the planning table at Hitler's headquarters in East Prussia. It was accidentally pushed further under the table, however, so that when it exploded Hitler was partly shielded. This saved his life. Thousands were arrested after this incident and hundreds, including von Stauffenberg, were executed.

D-DAY: DELIVERANCE OF EUROPE

THE NORMANDY INVASION: 6 JUNE 1944

As dawn broke on 6 June 1944, 6,000 Allied ships lay off the coast of Normandy in the biggest ever sea-borne invasion. Overhead, thousands of British and American aircraft swarmed over the French coastline to pound the enemy's defences, whilst airborne troops parachuted behind German lines to cause havoc and disruption.

It was one of the best-kept secrets of the war and security was tight. The Germans were convinced that the invasion would take place at the narrowest stretch of the channel – the Pas de Calais, opposite the English port of Dover. The Allies did all they could to make the Germans think they were right. Dummy landing craft were stationed all the way along the River Thames. Radio signals gave the impression that a force was being assembled for this destination. Five weeks after the D-day landings, the Germans were still convinced that the Normandy landings were a decoy to throw them off the scent.

That day, 250,000 soldiers stormed ashore along a 60-mile stretch of well-defended beaches. They faced formidable obstacles. Field Marshall von Runsted, the German commander responsible for the defence of France, Belgium and Holland, had more than half a million men under his command for the task. The beaches were packed with clever death traps to kill and maim an invading army. Every 1,000 metres, concrete pillboxes bristled with anti-tank guns, flame-throwers and machine-guns, manned by 50 to 200 men.

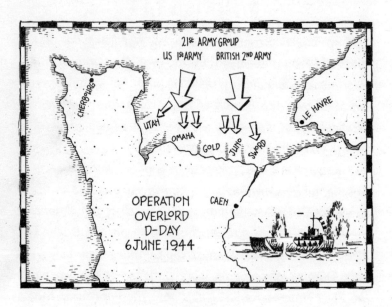

Operation Overlord.

Further inland, gun batteries were built to pound troop ships, whilst panzer divisions waited to spring on the Allies and throw them back into the sea should they break through.

Amongst those that hit the beaches on that longest of days was Company Sergeant Major Stan Hollis of the 6th battalion The Green Howards, a famous regiment in the British army. This is the story of what happened to one man on that fateful day.

Date: 6 June 1944
Place: Gold Beach, Normandy, France

As Dawn Breaks

Sergeant Stan Hollis took a quick look round at the men of D company who packed the landing craft. Bullets whined overhead and thumped into the side of the boat. Aircraft droned overhead. Artillery fire stabbed the sky. Oily smoke plumed from burning wrecks and caught in the back of the soldiers' throats.

As each man faced the likelihood of a sudden and violent death, most retreated into their private thoughts and fears. Some prayed silently, others thought of their families or tried to control their trembling. Many were seasick and longed for the land – no matter what it would bring.

The Landing Craft Assault bucked wildly in the swell of the sea. Water swept over the bows, but between the showers of spray that stung the eyes the thin, grey coastline of France gradually emerged into recognizable

Troops loading a landing craft aboard a ship.

buildings and clumps of trees. This was what all their training had been leading to. The aerial photographs that Stan and his men had studied for months were now taking shape before their eyes. From the edge of the beach, a thin track ran up to a house with a circular drive and beyond to the rise of a hill where their main objective lay – the gun battery at Mont Fleury. Their view then disappeared into the haze of open country.

Amazingly, they were right on target. As the LCA closed in on the shore, Stan was aware of an unsettling and eerie silence. The roar of shells from the bombarding ships offshore had fallen silent and, as yet, the German defences were not replying. He knew that this was only a lull and once the Germans returned to their guns all hell would break out. He could not shake one thought from his mind. The photographs had revealed what looked like a pillbox on the sea wall. It was well sited. From its vantage point it could send a deadly arc of fire along the beach.

'They need to be kept busy or my boys will be slaughtered,' Stan thought to himself. Taking a machine-gun from one of the men he balanced the weapon on the ramp of the landing craft and sent several bursts of fire in the general direction of the pillbox. The lurching of the landing craft made aiming difficult but he hoped that it would at least persuade the Germans to keep their heads down. As the craft neared the beach, Stan cupped his hand beneath the barrel to support its weight, quite forgetting in the tension of the moment that the barrel would still be hot. A searing burn printed itself across the palm of his hand.

'My first wound in this battle and it's self-inflicted. Sometimes you forget the most obvious things in the "heat" of battle.' He smiled wryly to himself at his own joke but at least it had the positive effect of calming some of his fears.

The landing craft hit the beach with a jolt, throwing a few of the men off balance. The ramp crashed down and the men piled out. They were soon waist-deep in ice-cold water. Weighted down with equipment, some fell face down into the water and drowned.

Stan snapped into action. Followed by three machine-gunners and three mortar-men, he raced for the high water mark, where his squad were supposed to lay down a smoke-screen to cover the rest of the soldiers as they scrambled up the beach. There was no need. Exploding bombs had already created an oily curtain of smoke that hung in strands across the beach.

British troops landing on a beach in Normandy.

Looking back to the shoreline, Stan kept his eye on the remaining landing craft. One driver had driven his vehicle with such force at the shore that its nose had become securely stuck in the sand. As the driver pressed harder on the accelerator to free the vehicle it had the opposite effect. Instead of forcing itself free, the tail began to swing round – straight towards a mine attached to a pole. The ramp should have come down when the vehicle hit the beach but this did not happen. Instead, the men were frozen in the safety of their metal shell.

At great personal risk, Stan jumped to his feet. He knew his voice would not carry above the din of battle but nevertheless he shouted to them, whilst waving his arms in a frenzy of warning. At first it had no effect. The tail was spinning ever nearer to destruction.

Only inches from the mine, however, one of the crew woke from his frozen state and gave the ramp a violent kick. Down it crashed and the men tumbled out, racing up to the ridge of sand that marked the high water limit.

There was no time to stop. The ridge of sand only gave temporary safety. Stan waved his men on. They must not become stranded on the beach. To do so would only allow the Germans to counter-attack and throw them back into the sea. But they needed to break through a line of hedge and bramble that ran parallel to the beach. Once through this obstacle they could then storm their main objective: the Mont Fleury gun battery.

Stan squirmed through a gap in the hedge and, emerging on the other side, he headed for the house with the circular drive. A burst of automatic fire crashed out from the area of the house and two men close to him fell wounded.

First Action

Stan gritted his teeth. 'Unless these guns are silenced,' he thought, 'the rest of D company has no chance of destroying the Mont Fleury battery. They'll be shot in the back!'

Stan, accompanied by Major Ronnie Lofthouse, crept up to the wall that surrounded the house, whilst two platoons raced past up the track to open the assault on the Mont Fleury battery. Major Lofthouse inched his head above the wall and spotted the source of the fire. A field gun was just visible amongst the bushes. The Germans had now turned their gun so that it was firing at the two platoons.

'There's a pillbox in there, Sergeant Major.' Major Lofthouse pointed to a clump of bushes about fifty metres to the right, just beyond the end of the wall.

Without waiting for further orders, Stan took off in a frontal assault on the enemy position. The Germans swung the gun round and began opening fire on him. Stan tried to weave and dart to make himself a difficult target. Bullets kicked up spurts of dust all around him but, miraculously, none of them hit him. Within seconds, he had reached the concrete wall and, without pausing, pushed the muzzle of his gun through the firing slit, spraying bullets into the black interior. Then he scrambled on to the top of the pillbox, lay down, unpinned a grenade and 'posted' it through the firing slit. A muffled bang was followed by a cloud of dust blown out of the metal door at the back entrance of the pillbox. Jumping down into the trench at the rear, he burst through the door. Two dead Germans were sprawled across the dirt floor, whilst the others, too dazed or wounded to put up any further resistance, surrendered.

British commandos push ashore.

Emerging back into the sunlight, Stan noticed that the trench he was in ran on for a further 100 metres, which led to another pillbox. He snapped another magazine into his Sten gun and advanced cautiously along the trench. As he approached the remaining pillbox the German defenders poured out. He stopped and pointed the muzzle of his gun at the bewildered Germans. His determined stance persuaded them that further resistance was useless and they put their hands up in surrender.

A few moments later, Sergeant Hollis reappeared on the track, leading a line of 25–30 prisoners, which he shepherded towards the beach patrols.

Meanwhile, the battery at Mont Fleury had taken such a heavy pounding that the German defenders had decided to abandon their position. As the Allied troops began to move further inland, however, German resistance began to pick up and a number of officers and men were killed. When Lieutenant Kirkpatrick was shot, Platoon 16 became leaderless and CSM Stan Hollis was ordered to assume command.

The Farmhouse

By mid-afternoon, D company had reached the village of Crepon and was pushing beyond en route for Bayeux. To the left of the main road from the village an old stone farmhouse dominated the route inland.

'An excellent place for snipers to hide,' thought Stan, 'but dangerous to clear. Sensitive trigger fingers could kill or wound my men as rooms are searched and doors kicked open.'

Stealthily, Stan's platoon set about searching the house, moving cautiously from one room to the next. The sergeant's ears were alert to the slightest sound and he was convinced that he heard a trickle of loose plaster hit the floor in one room. Bursting into the room, his gun was cocked to fire. He expected to be met by gunfire but the huddled shape he saw in the corner was too small to be a soldier. The figure turned its head and two frightened eyes stared at the sergeant. Stan pulled up his gun and gave the boy a toothy grin. A less experienced soldier might not have taken the chance but Stan would have found it impossible to live with himself if he had killed this innocent boy.

Not satisfied with merely clearing the farmhouse, Stan began to search the rest of the farm to ensure that no Germans were in hiding to wreak havoc behind the British lines. He had a healthy respect for the German soldier. Most were brave; some were fanatical and would willingly lay down their lives for the Fatherland. Stan moved gingerly down an alleyway at the back of the farm and, just as he was about to turn the corner, there was a loud crack of rifle fire. A bullet just missed the end of his nose and gouged out a piece of masonry centimetres from his face.

Stan fell flat on the ground and scanned the hedge ahead. About fifty metres away, a couple of dogs were wagging their tails and jumping around near a gap in the leafy cover. 'They can't be doing that without a reason. There must be someone there that the dogs have got used to,' reasoned Stan, 'and that must be the German gunners.'

Stan raced back to the road where he collected a **PIAT** anti-tank gun and ordered two Bren gunners to follow him. Meanwhile, the rest of his command was to draw the Germans' fire from the opposite direction.

Stan fell flat on his stomach and crawled through a patch of rhubarb to get a good sighting of the field gun. He took aim. But no covering fire erupted to distract the field gun. All his men had been wounded or killed by an alert enemy, but he was not to know this at the time. He opened fire but, to his horror, the round fell short. The Germans were now alerted to the sergeant's attack and turned their field gun in his direction. He could clearly see the black hole of the muzzle pointing directly at him, less than one hundred metres away.

Then there was a shattering explosion which deafened him. Seconds before, he had closed his eyes, expecting to die, but instead, the shell whistled over his head and slammed into the house behind him.

'To hell with this; I'm getting out of here.' Shouting to the two Bren gunners to follow him, Stan crawled back through the rhubarb patch to the cover of the wall. Reaching the road and D company, he reported back to Major Lofthouse, who decided that as the gun was no immediate threat to the operation it could be safely left to be 'mopped-up' by another patrol.

Their conversation was interrupted by the sound of machine-gun fire from the farmhouse. Stan looked around for the two Bren gunners and then realized to his horror that they had not heard him and had been left behind at the farmhouse. Snatching a Bren gun for himself, he sprinted back along the alleyway that ran alongside the wall. Reaching the end, he did not stop to take cover but raced into the orchard, shooting from the hip and screaming at the two men to get out. He stopped about fifty metres from the field gun, springing bullets in that direction until the two Bren gunners could make a hurried retreat. Miraculously, none of them were harmed.

The 6th Green Howards continued their advance until, as night began to fall, a halt was called. Sergeant Hollis slumped to the ground, loosened the straps of his helmet and pushed it back from his forehead. He ran through the actions of the day in his mind; his own narrow escapes from death, and remembered those who had not been so lucky. What he did not know was that he had been recommended for the highest honour in the British army – the Victoria Cross – the only soldier to be so decorated on D-day.

Company Sergeant Major Stan Hollis survived the war and many years later returned to the farmhouse where he had carried out his heroic action. To his great surprise the ten-year old boy, Monsieur Lahaye, was now the owner of the farm. Having shared that terrible moment of war, they greeted each other as long-lost friends.

FIGHTING FACTS

After D-Day the Allies began to force the Germans to retreat from their occupied territories. This marked the beginning of the end of the war.

The Atlantic Wall

After 1942, when the tide of war was beginning to turn against Germany, Hitler gave orders for concrete defences to be built along the European coast. The toughest defences were placed along the Pas de Calais. Field Marshal Rommel was placed in charge and was not impressed with what he found. In some cases the Germans had only erected balsa screens propped up by concrete walls to trick the Allies!

Fooling the Enemy

The Allies knew they had more chance of winning if they could fool the Germans into thinking they were going to land elsewhere. Operation Fortitude was the plan to persuade the Germans that the Allies were going to land at the nearest point to England – the Pas de Calais. A fic-

Rommel inspecting part of the Atlantic Wall.

titious army was created in Scotland to suggest that Norway might be invaded. More fictitious armies were created with dummy tanks and landing craft mushrooming along the banks of the river Thames.

The code name for the invasion of Normandy was Operation Overlord and Operation Neptune was the code name for the naval assault. Petrol was to be supplied through an underwater pipeline from England – Operation Pluto. There were also code names for the five groups of forces landing on the beaches – Utah, Omaha, Gold, Juno and Sword.

Imagine the horror of the D-Day planners when a crossword appeared in the *Daily Telegraph* containing the words 'Pluto', 'Overlord' and 'Omaha'! The crossword compiler received a visit from the Secret Service but, they concluded, it had been no more than a frightening coincidence.

The Invasion Force
Throughout May 1944 the south of England became one huge military camp.

Operation Overlord D- Day 6 June 1944

Troops

	Infantry Divisions	Armoured Divisions	Airborne Divisions	Total per country
United States	13	5	2	20
British	8	4	2	14
Canadian		1		1
French		1		1
Polish		1		1
Total	21	12	4	37

Air Forces

Heavy Bombers	3,958
Medium and light	1,234
Fighter bombers	<u>4,709</u>
	9,901

Naval Forces

Battleships	7
Monitors	2
Cruisers	23
Gunboats	2
Destroyers	93

Sloops	15
Escorts	<u>142</u>
	284

Landing Craft	4,308

Special Type Equipment

LVTs	470
DD Tanks	514
DUKWs	<u>2,583</u>
	3,567

Officers and Men

Air	659,554
Land	1,931,885
Sea	<u>285,000</u>
	2,876,439

Pinned on the Beach

Five groups landed on the beaches. Only on Omaha beach did the Allies experience real difficulties, with 1,000 dead and 2,000 wounded.

Bob Edlin, an American infantryman, was at Omaha beach:

I saw one of the sergeants there and his left thumb was gone but he didn't look as if he was hurt too badly so I called his name and told him to get up and come with us. But when I got closer I saw there was blood all

*over his back . . . and then I was hit by machine-gun
fire in the left leg and the pain was terrible. It knocked
me down and I thought, 'Well, I haven't been here ten
minutes and I've already got a Purple Heart.'*

Inventions That Won the Day

Operation Mulberry

The raid on Dieppe in 1943 had made it clear that it
would not be easy to capture an undamaged port. To
solve this particular problem over one hundred giant
concrete blocks were towed across the channel and
positioned off Gold and Omaha beaches to form
artificial harbours.

Operation Pluto

The problem of how to supply petrol was solved with
underground supply lines.

Many other inventions were designed to make the
invasion a success. Tanks were fitted with giant flails at
the front to explode mines.

Weapons That Won the Beaches

P-51 Mustang fighter plane

This made an important contribution to the successful
Normandy landings by winning air control from Germany. It was one of the most remarkable aircraft of the
war. It was capable of flying to Berlin and back with
long-range drop tanks and out-gunning every Luftwaffe

Aerial view of Mulberry harbour.

opponent. Normally armed with six .5 machine-guns, it had a top speed of 475 mph (764 kph) and could fly as high as 42,000 feet (12,801 m).

Churchill Crocodile

This was among the best-known of the armoured division's 'funnies'. This tank could spit out a jet of burning fuel to clear out enemy positions 40–50 yards ahead of it.

17 pounder anti-tank gun

This was the best Allied anti-tank gun of the war, capable of penetrating 149 mm armour at 100 yards.

DUKW (Duplex-Drive amphibious truck)

Known as the 'Duck', this amphibious vehicle could operate on land and sea.

PIAT (Projector Infantry anti-tank)

A hand-held anti-tank weapon, which at close quarters could disable a tank.

Bazooka

An American infantry anti-tank weapon.

Bren Gun

.303 light machine-gun widely used in the British army.

ESCAPE
FROM
ARNHEM

BATTLE BRIEFING

Two weeks after the Allied landings in France in June 1944, a bridgehead of sixty miles had been secured along the Normandy coastline. But due to skilful German defence the breakout from Normandy was painfully slow. At the end of July, however, the Americans succeeded in smashing through the German lines and poured into the rest of France, whilst the British army broke through at Caen and fought their way into southern Holland.

The Allies were now poised along the river Rhine at the borders of Germany itself. One big push and the war could be brought to an end. But the Germans, though reeling before the attacks, were now more ferocious in defence of their homeland. The Dutch countryside was flooded by Germans to slow down the Allied advance. Furthermore, the British and the Americans were far in advance of their supply lines.

Montgomery's plan for Operation Market Garden.

If only, the Allied generals thought, they could snatch the bridges across the Rhine, then they could drive into the heart of Germany and bring the war in Europe to a quick end.

General Montgomery came up with a bold plan. He would land a '60-mile carpet' of airborne troops behind enemy lines. They would secure all the bridges for the Allies to cross, including the one farthest away which crossed the Rhine itself, at the town of Arnhem. It seemed a dazzling opportunity and the go-ahead was given for the plan to be put into effect.

Parachute drop over Arnhem.

But it all went horribly wrong. The Germans were waiting, and waiting in strength. British troops were surrounded and killed or captured after heroic stands. A few stragglers attempted the impossible – to escape back to the Allied lines. One such soldier was Colonel Graeme Warrack, a doctor with the 1st Airborne Division at Arnhem.

Date: September 1944
Place: Appledoorn hospital barracks, near Arnhem, Holland

In Hiding

There was nothing for it. Doctor Graeme Warrack, Colonel with the 1st Airborne Division, decided that his first duty was to look after the wounded. These men he was now in charge of were all that was left from the force of 10,000 British soldiers dropped or landed sixty miles behind German lines to capture key bridges. True, over 2,000 had escaped back to the British lines, but the

Aerial view of the bridge at Arnhem.

British troops fighting in the rubble of Arnhem.

slaughter had been terrible. Only 600 had made it to the farthest bridge at Arnhem. Most had never even seen the bridge at all but had been trapped in a couple of square miles where they were shot to pieces by German machine-guns and tanks.

Armed with the only the lightest of weapons, they had fought against 60-ton Tiger tanks until forced to continue the fight from the cellars of shattered houses. Hungry and weary, they fought to the last man or, as they ran out of ammunition, grudgingly surrendered. It had been a gamble to end the war swiftly but it was a risk that hadn't paid off.

Now the survivors were prisoners of the Germans and as Graeme tended the injured his mind turned to thoughts of escape. Once the sick were well enough to be transported to prison camps in Germany he was determined to make a run for it. He was not alone. Many of the other doctors and less seriously injured were hatching escape plans too. It was only 40 kilometres to the front line, although the route was crawling with German soldiers and anyone escaping was likely to be shot. But no one wanted to spend the rest of the war rotting in a prison camp.

Each day more and more British soldiers, as soon as they felt well enough to make a bid for freedom, disappeared from the hospital wards. Hiding in bushes, hayricks and outhouses, they waited until dark and then slipped off into the surrounding countryside.

Unfortunately, Graeme had few advantages as an escapee. He was the senior medical officer and would be missed immediately. He was also very tall – over six foot – and therefore easy to spot. He decided that his only chance was to go into hiding and wait for the British advance to free him.

Graeme searched every nook and cranny of the hospital until, one morning before he began his ward rounds, he sat staring at the ceiling, wondering where he could hide. And then it became blindingly obvious to him. In the rambling warren of the hospital there were bound to be twists, turns and corners in the roof space where he might remain undiscovered.

Once the idea was fixed in his head it didn't take him long to find a hatch in the ceiling near his office. In the days that followed, he stocked the roof space above his office with water, food, blankets, candles and civilian clothing until there were enough provisions to last a long wait.

In October, Graeme waved goodbye to the last of the soldiers who were now well enough to be taken to prison of war camps in Germany. He turned back to the hospital, climbed the stairs to his office and made straight for the trapdoor. Glancing round the office to make sure he'd not been seen, he slid the hatch shut and plunged himself into the gloom and dust of the loft. He would not have a long wait, he thought, for he could already hear the boom of artillery guns a little way to the south. And, with luck, the Germans may think he had been evacuated with the rest of the wounded.

But the Allies didn't arrive. Days turned into weeks. The Germans dynamited canals, making it difficult for the Allies to advance across waterlogged fields. Meanwhile, Graeme was running out of food and water. Terrified that a wrong footfall or a sudden uncontrollable sneeze would betray his presence, he decided that he would have to leave his hiding place.

On 29 October Graeme Warrack opened the hatch of his cramped hiding place. It was a brilliantly moonlit night. He tried to keep to the deep shadows as he edged his way down the stairs to the courtyard below. At first he could barely move his legs. He'd had no exercise cooped up in the tiny roof space. Reaching the lower floor, Graeme glanced through the office window. There appeared to be no sentry on duty outside. He eased the catch free and slowly swung the window open when, to his horror, he caught sight of the shadow of a German soldier less than a metre from him. Graeme was fortunate that the guard had his back to him – this was the probable reason he had not been heard.

Graeme slunk back into the shadows and dropped to the floor below the window. Straining his ears to the utmost, he heard the guard rub his hands for warmth against the frosty night air. Less than a minute later the man stamped his feet and marched off into the night. Graeme could hear his heart pounding in his chest. That had been too close to bear. He blew out a gasp of relief.

Gradually, the guard's footsteps faded into the night. When he could hear them no more, Graeme eased himself up to the window ledge and then cautiously peered out. The guard was 20 metres away and about to turn a corner. That would be his moment to dash across the courtyard.

A small cloud scudded across the moon and plunged the courtyard into darkness. Graeme swung his stiff legs over the sill and gently pushed the window shut behind him. He had only seconds to cross the rain-soaked courtyard before the moon would illuminate everything again. He checked the guard had disappeared and then sprinted across the clearing. But the cobbles were slippery from the rain and as he neared the shadows on the far side of the courtyard between two buildings his feet slid from beneath him. He began to topple backwards but saved himself from clattering to the ground by grasping at a metal railing.

Pausing for breath, he listened for signs that he had been discovered. He expected a guard to come running at any moment, gun blazing. But there was not a sound. So far so good. Graeme studied the way ahead. A further 30 metres would take him to the next deep shadow, close by the stable. Again, he waited until a cloud blotted out the moonlight before dashing across the rest of the courtyard. Pressing himself against the wall, he accidentally scraped the lower masonry with his boot. The sound was barely audible but to him it felt like a thunderclap. Inside the stable, a horse whinnied and shook its head, rattling its halter.

Graeme was sure the noise from the horse would arouse the Germans' suspicions. He screwed his eyes tightly shut. But the noise had gone unnoticed. Opening his eyes, he could now see that he was only metres away from the fence that surrounded the hospital grounds. Beyond was freedom, but also danger.

Graeme felt his way along the fence, searching for a way under or over. The top had been renewed with razor-sharp wire, so Graeme concentrated on finding a slack piece of fence which might allow him to slide underneath. But there seemed no easy way through. Desperation welled up inside him.

Dropping on to his hands and knees, Graeme crawled along the grassy embankment until he came to a clump of trees and bushes, through which the fence ran. He noticed that the roots of one of the trees had grown through the soil and formed a ridge which had bent the bottom of the fence upward. This must not have been so apparent when the wire had been strung in the summer but now that the shrubbery was dying back the roots had pushed the wire up by about 18 centimetres above the ground.

'Just as well I've been on a diet,' Graeme mused to himself. Wriggling on his back, he cleared the wire. Clear of the hospital, his fear returned. This was only the first step in his escape bid. It would be a long and dangerous trek to the Rhine.

In the dark it was easy to get lost but he knew if he could find his way to the railway line at Eade, this would guide him south to the Allied lines. The railway track lay some 18 kilometres away and this would be the next hazardous part of his journey. He had heard that a group of British paratroopers were hiding out there and if he could make it to them, then they all stood a chance of crossing the Rhine to their own side.

Graeme walked through the night and then hid in a small wood at daybreak. The sudden forced activity of the night before, after weeks in his cramped hiding place, made his legs ache. As he lay in his nest of fallen autumn leaves a sudden downpour soaked him to the skin. His lips chattered uncontrollably and he tugged his jacket tightly round his body to keep warm.

A Stroke of Good Luck

As night fell, Graeme set off once more. He was desperately thirsty. He plucked frost-covered oak leaves from the trees and sucked them to quench his thirst.

Deep into the night, he came across a farmhouse. He knew he needed help but contact with anyone was dangerous, even with the Dutch. Some might help, others might hand him in. Most would just tell him to clear off. Anyone caught helping British soldiers was likely to be shot on the spot.

Graeme made his way along a garden fence until he came to a gap in the hedge, where he could see a cottage about 30 metres away. A warm pool of light bathed a patch of garden beneath the window. In the cold, bleak night it seemed so inviting, so irresistible. He decided to risk it and hoped that the people inside would be friendly.

Creeping to the window, Graeme peered in. Two Dutch women were sitting at a kitchen table. Graeme tapped on the window, trying not to panic them. Three short taps, concluded by one long one. Everyone in occupied Europe knew what this meant. It was Morse code – V for victory, used by the BBC as the signature for their broadcasting services to the people of Europe.

Graeme had struck lucky. The Reint family had contacts with the Resistance.

Nevertheless, Tineke Reint was startled when she opened the door. After weeks of cramped confinement, Graeme Warrack looked more like a tramp than a colonel from an elite paratroop regiment. Unshaven, shrouded in a blanket and with a dirt-streaked face and red-rimmed eyes, he looked like a criminal on the run. Tineke would have had just cause to slam the door in his face. But what caught the Dutch partisan's gaze was the red paratrooper's beret that Graeme had deliberately worn so as not to be shot as a spy.

'Come, come quickly.' Tineke shepherded Graeme in as she quickly scanned the neighbourhood to make sure they had not been seen. 'Sit,' Tineke commanded Graeme in the little English she knew. 'Eat.'

After a simple meal, which the starving Dutch could barely provide, Graeme was taken into the woods nearby and hidden in an underground dugout lined with logs. After living in his cramped prison for so long it was a luxury to be able to stretch his legs. That night he slept soundly, feeling warm and safe for the first time in many months.

Familiar and reassuring sounds filtered into his hideout. The low hum of cars that passed on the nearby road, the chatter of couples walking through the woods. All these sounds gave him a sense of well-being. But as the days passed he became increasingly anxious, not just for his own safety but for that of the Reint family. If caught, the Germans would show no mercy. The men in the family would be shot immediately and the women dragged off to concentration camps.

The Visitor

Graeme's nerves were becoming increasingly frayed. About two weeks after he'd arrived there, as he lay in the straw a sliver of light pierced the gloom, sending a whirl of dust motes dancing in the pale autumn light. A shadow slipped into the dugout, holding a finger to his lips.

'Good evening, Colonel Warrack. I am Piet von Arnhem. I am pleased to say that you will be going home. You will be joining some of your comrades soon and be taken across the river Ede to your friends.'

Graeme felt a huge weight had been lifted from his shoulders. But as the excitement surged through his body at the thought of escape, his fear returned.

'But what of the enemy patrols? We'll be like sitting ducks.'

Piet looked puzzled, not understanding the term 'sitting ducks'.

'The Germans will spot us easily on the water,' Graeme explained.

'No, Colonel. Your soldiers are crossing the river on daring raids almost every night. A short while ago 150 men were helped across to their own lines in this way.' Piet tried to reassure Graeme and sounded very confident, but Graeme was riddled with doubts.

Another Night Escape

Graeme pressed his face to the earth in a shallow ditch whilst bullets whined overhead and thudded into the soft earth by his feet. He could hear grunts and cries of pain from fallen comrades. Sten guns stuttered; grenades exploded, sending showers of earth down on his head.

The carefully laid plan for their mass escape had fallen apart. The Germans were everywhere. One or two men were killed, several wounded and only seven men had made it across the Rhine. Graeme was not one of them.

He wormed his way on his stomach into a nearby clump of trees as the noise of the pursuing Germans grew fainter. They were focusing on the river where some men had attempted a crossing. Graeme darted from bush to bush and as he left the riverbank, the commotion grew fainter and fainter.

There was nothing else left to do but to make his way back to the Reints. He made it safely and joined an American pilot and a Dutch civilian in the familiar underground dugout.

Free At Last

In the first week of February, more than three months after his escape from the hospital at Appledoorn,

Warrack stepped into a wobbling canoe with two Dutch companions. Their plan was to paddle some 20 kilometres down canals and tributaries until they could cross the Rhine. The whole area bristled with defences. Machine-gun posts lay hidden along the riverbanks, searchlights swept the river.

The last stage of the journey was the most terrifying. By this time they were down to one canoe, the others having sunk after becoming waterlogged. A strong wind had whipped up waves and they were only making slow headway.

As they paddled, Graeme's hands had become increasingly bloodied with the effort. His blisters had burst and the tender skin beneath was soon beaded with blood. But they'd gone too far to turn back. As they drifted down a narrow stream a voice barked out, 'Halt! Who goes there?'

The voice was – yes – the voice was speaking English. They'd made it!

FIGHTING FACTS

A Bridge Too Far?

Field Marshall Bernard Montgomery, the hero of El Alamein, was convinced that the war could be brought quickly to an end if the Allied forces could capture the bridges through Holland and over the Rhine into

The bridge at Arnhem.

Germany. The US 101 were to capture the Sindhoven and Uden canal bridges, whilst the US 82 was to take the Maas and Waal bridges.

Most dangerous of all, the British 1st Airborne Division were to be dropped 60 miles behind the enemy lines at a little town called Arnhem, deep inside enemy-held territory.

Montgomery's Deputy-Commander, Lieutenant General 'Boy' Browning, however, thought the plan too risky and warned Montgomery, 'I think we may be going one bridge too far.' He was right.

Dutch Underground Resistance
The Reint family was one among many Dutch people who formed resistance groups after their country's

defeat in 1940. Like other resistors in occupied countries they organized sabotage against the hated enemy and sent valuable information about German troop movements to Britain.

Unfortunately, the Germans were lucky enough to capture a radio transmitter and codes in 1941. Sending fake messages to British Intelligence they lured some supplies and agents straight into their hands. After this disaster British Intelligence became very suspicious of any information they received from Holland. It was to prove their undoing at Arnhem. Despite repeated warnings from the Dutch resistance that German panzer divisions were stationed near Arnhem, Montgomery refused to call a halt to his operation.

Caught in the Crossfire

Many civilians were caught up in the middle of the fighting. Private Tucker of the Parachute regiment described one tough old lady who refused to budge from her house:

> We hadn't got far when this young soldier came rushing in to say that there was an old lady in one of the back bedrooms and she was refusing to go. In the end she stayed and the young soldier risked his life a dozen times to feed her. All through the terrible fighting to come, she remained in that back bedroom never turning a hair when all the shells were crashing all around us. Astounded by her courage, it was only

afterwards that I learned she'd been deaf as a post
all along.

Escape

Exhausted, hungry and attacked on all sides by flame-throwers and tanks, the parachute regiment hung on to their positions on the bridge at Arnhem for eight days before surrendering to the Germans. Survivors split up into small groups and set out along different routes to make their way back to the British lines.

> *Our major was an old hand. He led the way and linked*
> *the party together by getting everyone to hold the tail*
> *of the parachutist's smock of the man in front of him*
> *so our column resembled some children's game. The*
> *worst moment was waiting by the riverside (Lower*
> *Rhine) till our turn came to be ferried across. The*
> *Germans kept sending up flares and we had to lie flat*
> *and motionless on a soaking field with cold rain*
> *drizzling down.*

Was Arnhem a Success?

The Allies claimed it was because they had captured a number of bridges through Holland. However, they had failed to hang on to the bridge at Arnhem. This was vital to the 'dagger thrust' at Germany.

Once the airborne troops had landed the Germans knew to concentrate their counter-attack along the route attempted by the relieving second army. The

Sherman tanks went to the aid of the British forces but they were sitting targets as they travelled through the flat Dutch countryside on the raised roads.

THE BATTLE FOR BURMA

BATTLE BRIEFING

The Japanese menace had been steadily growing in the Far East throughout the 1930s. Dominated by the army, the Japanese government was forced to accept the imperial ambitions of its generals. Most of China fell to their military forces and they looked to expand their empire further by grabbing the colonies of the French and British in the Far East. After 1940 only the United States stood in their way, for Britain was fighting for her own survival and France had been defeated by Germany.

Whilst discussions were taking place between Japan and America, the Japanese launched a massive surprise attack on the American naval base at Pearl Harbor in Hawaii on 7 December 1941. Three hundred and fifty-three Japanese planes, launched from six aircraft carriers, destroyed six battleships, three cruisers, three destroyers and 149 planes.

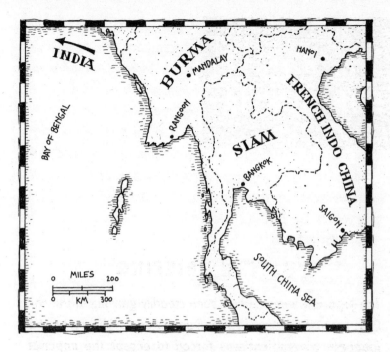

Burma.

Over 4,000 American soldiers and civilians were killed or wounded in the raid. The American Pacific fleet was all but paralysed. Left with only the shattered remnants of a fleet to oppose them, the Japanese were free to spread across the Asian mainland and the Pacific.

As a result of the attack on Pearl Harbor, the USA officially declared war on Japan on 10 December 1941. Then Germany and Italy, Japan's allies, declared war on the USA. What had been mainly a European war had now truly become a world war.

225

The Japanese lost little time in attacking the British Empire in the Far East. On 11 December 1941 Malaya was invaded. Four days later, Japanese troops invaded Burma, with the intention of sweeping on to India, the 'jewel' of the British Empire.

The British were in a perilous position. Not only had they lost vast areas of their empire to the Japanese but also many Indian subjects were demanding independence from Britain. For this reason, the loyalty of thousands of Indians who served in the British Indian army could now no longer be taken for granted.

The British position became even more desperate. On 15 February 1942, the great British naval base at Singapore fell to Japanese forces. There seemed little that could be done to stop the advancing tide. Throughout early 1942 the Imperial Japanese armies made a series of rapid gains. They captured many of the islands across the western Pacific and even threatened Australia itself. By 20 May 1942 all of Burma was in Japanese hands and they were poised to strike into India.

The British decided to try and hold the frontier fast, whilst sending guerrilla troops to fight deep inside enemy territory. By the end of the year, after fierce fighting, the Allies began to win the struggle against the Japanese. By May 1945, Rangoon, the capital of Burma, was recaptured. In the Pacific, American and Allied forces retook Japanese-held islands. The cost of these campaigns in human life was huge.

In order to end the war quickly and save the lives of further Allied soldiers, it was decided to use a secret weapon. On

6 August 1945 an atom bomb was dropped on the town of Hiroshima in Japan, causing thousands of deaths and injuries. After a second atomic bomb was used on Nagasaki, the Japanese surrendered on 14 August 1945.

Most attention was focused on the war in Europe, and so many of the soldiers who fought in the Allied armies in the Far East have come to regard themselves as the 'Forgotten Army'. One such man was Martin McLane. What is frequently forgotten as well is that many of the soldiers came from many different parts of the world – from Africa, the West Indies and from India itself. Rifleman Lachhiman Gurung was one such soldier. Born in Nepal, he came from a long line of people who had fought courageously in the British Army.

The Forgotten Army

The Meeting

The Royal Chelsea Hospital sits near the banks of the River Thames in London. Strictly speaking it isn't a hospital at all but a home for retired soldiers built by Charles II over three hundred years ago. And so it remains today – much larger than when it was first built, but still carrying on the traditions of the past. There are over 700 pensioners in the Royal Hospital, each one with a fascinating story to tell. Many are in their eighties and nineties and when they pass away, their stories will be lost, their histories forgotten.

I first came across Martin McLane, one of the pensioners, in a magazine article about the war in Burma. Martin's photograph was also there. Taken during World War II, the faded and dog-eared picture showed a stocky, well-built man. His hair was neatly groomed and a broad wave of moustache swept across his upper lip. The mouth gave a hint of a smile. But it was his eyes that caught my attention. They positively glittered with humour and intelligence. After an exchange of letters, I arranged to meet Martin.

After lunch Martin and I sat back in two comfortable armchairs. Resting his walking stick against the arm of the chair, he folded his hands together and began.

'So you want to hear about Burma. Well, there'll be things I'll tell you that you won't find in the history books.'

Setting Off

France and the retreat to Dunkirk was bad enough but there was worse to come when the Japanese began to attack us in the East and the 2nd battalion was given orders for overseas. We embarked on a troop train and were under strict orders not to leave the carriages. On 12 April, my birthday, we embarked on the *Empress of Canada*, a cruise liner converted to a troopship.

We steamed well out into the Atlantic to stay clear of submarines, and were escorted by destroyers and cruisers. The Mediterranean was too dangerous so we had to go right round Africa. What a welcome as we rounded the Cape. The docks of Capetown were lined with women singing a greeting and we were allowed four hours' leave.

Now Pat Brennan, my best friend, loved to gamble but he had no money. 'Lend me a few bob, Martin. There's a game going on over there.'

Of course, he lost everything, but he was a mate so there was no bad feeling. Years later Pat became an officer and we were still the best of friends, went everywhere together until we were both called into the commander's office one day and told the friendship had to end. You see, officers and men couldn't mix together socially. I didn't like it but that was the army. I guess they were afraid it would confuse everybody. You had to keep your distance.

You can imagine the next morning everyone was late back. They'd had such a good time ashore. Our thoughts began to turn to our destination. We still didn't know where it would be. That was a secret. If the enemy found out, the ship could have been sunk. But we had a pretty good idea. Singapore – the rumour spread around the ship. We knew the Japs had their eyes on the place. But we were wrong. Singapore fell and we arrived in India instead.

Into Battle

We weren't very welcome there. Many Indians were followers of Mahatma Gandhi who wanted the British to 'quit India' and for India to win her independence after being a British colony for nearly two hundred years.

Our job, as it gradually became clear, was to be

229

trained in jungle warfare. I'll tell you, the jungle is a frightening place. No sun penetrates so there's little light. The vegetation is thick and you never know where the enemy might be lying in wait for you. The Japanese, on the other hand, had adapted well. They'd built bunkers, covered with huge logs and earth. They could live on a handful of rice and were fanatical in attack; happy to lose their lives for their country.

Our soldiers were tough but even the best can be let down if they haven't the right equipment. For example, when we went into battle, we wore khaki Drill Battle Dress. It was sandy-coloured and quite unfit for jungle camouflage where we stood out distinctively. No effort was made to alter this. We even wore white vests and underwear, which meant if you took your tunic off, you became even more prominent against the dark greens of the jungle.

Just imagine the state we were in after six weeks of fighting in battle or lying in holes in the ground for pro-tection. We did have one spare kit but this was lost when the Japs overran Brigade Headquarters where they were stored. We also couldn't take hot showers when we were front-line troops. All we could do was use part of our water ration for washing. If we felt really scruffy, we'd pour some water into our mess tins, the same tin that we used for meals, and try to wash and shave in it. We must have stunk. It's surprising the Japs couldn't smell us coming!

Worse than the lack of proper camouflaged uniforms were the faulty weapons we were given. We'd been issued with a new type of Thompson sub-machine-gun and the men were keen to get their hands on what they thought was going to be a much better weapon. As a Company Sergeant Major – I'd been promoted by this time – I was due to get one but no instructions came with them.

'McLane,' the Company Commander barked, 'bring me my Thompson. I want to try it out.'

I handed him the weapon and we went down to the beach together so he could fire it into the sea. Steadying the gun against his hip, he let off one round. I looked in the direction it should have gone but couldn't spot the plume of water it should have made.

'Stop, sir!' I held my hand up. 'I don't like the sound of that shot.' It had sounded muffled.

'You're too cautious,' he replied. 'It's a new gun. Sounds different.'

He took aim once more and squeezed the trigger. BANG! My ears rang from the sound as I realized that the first round had stuck in the barrel. The second round hadn't a clear passage and the gun had burst apart. The Commander reeled back with the force of the explosion and fell to the ground unconscious. I dropped to my knees and scanned his body for wounds. Amazingly there were none. Gradually, his eyes flickered open and a few moments later he began to remember what had happened.

The army doesn't like to admit mistakes and the faulty Thompson machine-gun was said to be a freak and the others were fine. Yet no one was allowed to test them – with disastrous results, as I'll tell you.

The Attack

The officers decided that they would put in an attack on the Japanese positions. The sea was to our right whilst we were dug in flat lands partly covered by jungle. Immediately in front of our position were three dried-up river beds, carved out of the soft soil on the seaward side by the heavy monsoon rains. We couldn't outflank the Japanese and so had to meet them head on.

We had a special commando group in our battalion who went in first under cover of darkness. They were to cross a tidal river or *chung* down by the beach. They all had Thompson machine-guns, rifles and grenades and their faces were blackened.

I was detailed to the observation post in the front line to listen to the attack and judge how it was going. After a few moments I heard the thump of the grenades but I couldn't hear the rattle of automatic fire from the Thompsons. All of a sudden, the commando group came crashing back through the jungle, cursing and swearing. It was the Thompsons. They'd let us down again.

This was serious but it was wartime and there was no enquiry in case the soldiers lost confidence in their weapons. Well, we had no confidence at all. The army blamed the ammunition. Some said the American ammunition we were given wasn't waterproof. Others said it had been tampered with by anti-British Indians.

The attack was called off until new ammunition arrived but when it arrived it looked poor quality. Cheap, thin bright brass casings instead of bronze. Again our guns failed when we went into attack. It made me cry to see those brave young conscripts shattered by shrapnel. But I was told to press on with the attack. If the guns were defective then we were to use grenades. The carnage was terrible. Major Hurtman had been shot in the knee and couldn't move so I carried him to safety. I looked hard but there seemed to be no officer left unwounded and so I found myself in charge.

I decided to lead the men out, and all the time the Commanding Officer was complaining that we hadn't fought hard enough. But there were only fifteen men left out of a company of 90. The attack was a failure and there was no point in leading men to their deaths when all was hopeless.

Now, I've seen history books describe our efforts as weak-kneed but they weren't there. They don't understand that the monsoons had gouged the banks of the dried riverbeds until they were impossible to scale without ladders. Even then we had to carry 70 lb packs on our backs. Nor could we rely on our weapons or the ammunition. No, the battle in the Arakan was lost, not by the men but by faulty weapons and bad planning. But you don't always hear the history from the soldiers who fought the battles.

Rifleman Lachhiman Gurung VC
Date: 12/13 May 1945
Place: Taungdawn, the Irrawaddy River, Burma

A Proud Day

Rifleman Lachhiman Gurung stood to attention, trying to stand taller than his modest five feet. The sun was beating down on the parade ground at the Red Fort, Delhi, and although he'd stood to attention for well over an hour it didn't matter to him. Ringing the central square, regiments of the British Indian army and the British army stood rigidly in line. Brilliant red, green and gold flags fluttered alongside Union Jacks; cavalry horses gently pawed the ground or snorted in the heat of the day. It all looked magnificent.

He found it hard to believe but they were here to honour him – a Gurkha from a village deep in the remote Chitwan district of western Nepal. He was soon to be awarded the highest military honour in the British army – the Victoria Cross.

When he looked back over his life in the army he thought how lucky he'd been to get into the services at all due to his height – in peacetime he would have been rejected. But the demands of war and the shortage of soldiers had meant that the British army had had to lower their height standards. What Lachhiman lacked in height, however, he made up for in courage.

Lachhiman had enlisted in 1941, the lowest point in the war for Britain. With Europe under the heel of the Nazis, the Japanese had struck in the Far East. Malaya, Singapore and Burma had fallen and the Imperial Japanese armies were poised on the frontiers of India itself. Lachhiman was thrown into battle alongside Indian, British, East and West African, and Burmese soldiers in a desperate attempt to stem the tide of the Japanese advance.

But although the Japanese had been victorious, their supply lines were badly over-stretched and their attacks began to falter. But not before both sides had experienced some of the most bitter fighting of the war at the two Indian border stations of Imphal and Kohima. So close were the two armies at one point that at night, it was just possible to hear enemy troops breathing only a few feet away.

Behind the Japanese lines, Allied troops deep in Japanese-held land were causing havoc and devastation to railways and roads supplying the Japanese forces. The Japanese had no choice but to retreat. It had been a close fight. If the Japanese had broken through at Kohima then they could have flooded on to the plains of India and possibly linked-up with the German armies in the Caucasus in Russia.

But the battles on the borders of India had been deci-

A soldier covers his comrades
with a Bren Gun.

sive. The war was not over but it was the beginning of
the end for the Japanese Imperial armies.

A History of Heroes

Lachhiman came from a people who had always been
fighters. First recruited into the British army during the
reign of Queen Victoria in the mid-nineteenth century,
they earned a well-deserved reputation as loyal and
ferocious fighters. Born in remote villages of the
Himalayas in the kingdom of Nepal, they knew how to
survive under the most difficult conditions. Lachhiman
himself came from a long line of volunteers who had

served the British Empire and he wished to be part of the same tradition.

In March 1945 Lachhiman was posted to the 4th Battalion, 8th Gurkha Rifles in Burma. By May the Japanese forces were retreating down the Irrawaddy River that runs the whole length of the country. The jungle, swamp and mountain ranges of Burma were formidable obstacles in themselves. Dense foliage gave perfect cover for ambushes and meant every foot of land had to be hacked through. Nor would the Japanese give up

Ghurka soldiers after a battle with the
Japanese, on Linch Hill.

ground easily, sacrificing hundreds of men to delay the enemy advance. Each of their soldiers had a fanatical belief in their Emperor and was willing to die for him. The worst humiliation for a Japanese soldier was to be defeated and taken prisoner, for this brought shame on the man's family as well as himself. This explains why they fought so ferociously, with little regard for their own lives, and why they were often cruel to the prisoners they captured.

Stand and Fight

On 11 May, 'B' and 'C' Companies in Lachhiman's battalion were ordered to hold an important position astride a forest track on the west side of the river near to the village of Taungdaw. This track was vital to the Japanese breakout. Many of them had been cut off and were desperately trying to break through to escape capture. For three days and nights the Japanese launched attack after attack at British positions. But against well dug-in positions the Japanese attempts were suicidal and the hillside was soon littered with their dead. Again and again, they threw themselves across the clearings, only to be mown down by machine-guns.

The key position was held by No. 9 platoon almost 100 yards (91 m) forward of the remainder of the company. They were bearing the brunt of the attack. And in the most exposed position of all was Lachhiman's section. They were ordered to hold the line at all costs. They expected attacks at any time and all the time. Their nerves were taut and they scanned the undergrowth for any movement that might erupt into an attack.

The Japanese had switched their attacks to night in an attempt to both reduce casualties and to take the British by surprise. There was no moonlight to speak of and every rustle of bush and screech of animal grated the British soldiers' nerves.

At 1:20 in the morning about 200 enemy soldiers assaulted Lachhiman's section and he was in the front

A Gurkha soldier carries a wounded comrade
from the battlefield.

line. He understood well that if his trench were overrun it would open up the track behind him. This would allow the enemy to break through and overwhelm the rest of the two companies dug in along the hillside.

Lachhiman kept up a constant fire, stopping only once when a grenade bounced on the lip of his trench. He at once grasped the bomb and hurled it back in the direction of the enemy. No sooner had he done so than another landed in the trench at his feet. He picked this one up too and threw it back at the enemy.

The grenades fragmented in a blinding explosion. Screams of men in agony tore the night apart, but he had achieved his objective. Most of the Japanese in the vanguard of the attack had been killed.

Lachhiman slowly raised his eyes above the lip of the trench, only to see a third grenade bouncing towards him, only two feet away. As enemy bullets whined about his head, he reached out and took the grenade in his hand, stretching his arm back to throw it at the enemy when it exploded in his grasp. Lachhiman reeled back into the trench, his head pounding with the noise of the explosion. He could see that where his fingers should have been there was now only a bloody stump. Nor could he move his arm, which hung limp at his side. Because he'd been in a trench much of the explosion had also caught him in the face and streams of blood clouded his vision. For a brief moment he thought his life would soon come to an end.

He looked round for his two comrades but quickly realized that neither of them would be able to help him. Both had been badly wounded and lay writhing in agony at the bottom of the trench.

Lachhiman struggled to his feet and wiped the blood from his face with the back of his hand. He could feel only numbness in his right hand and arm, for the pain of his injuries had not begun to bite into his mind.

At the edge of the clearing, beyond the mounds of dead, the enemy were forming up again, shoulder to shoulder, for what seemed to be a final assault. Sheer weight of numbers would easily overrun Lachhiman's position and he could expect little help from the hard-pressed remainder of his section.

Rifleman Lachhiman Gurung steadied himself. He ignored his wounds and calmly but quickly began to reload his rifle with his left hand. Firing volley after volley, he kept up a steady and continuous rate of fire. Screaming and shouting, the Japanese lines faltered and then failed. They regrouped and charged again but nothing could unnerve Lachhiman as he kept up a hail of fire on the attacking, screaming hordes.

The Death Toll Mounts

Incredibly, Lachhiman stayed at his post for four hours, pouring a constant stream of fire on the enemy. The severely wounded rifleman propped himself up and calmly waited for each renewed attack, which he met with fire at point-blank range. He was determined that he would not give one inch of ground for the honour of his platoon and his ancestors.

The attack began to peter out after that, for even the Japanese could not endure such heavy losses and he heard them retreat through the undergrowth. He slumped back into the trench, barely able to stand after his constant efforts and from the loss of blood. He heard friendly voices as his head began to swim and he lost unconsciousness.

His rescuers could hardly believe their eyes. Eighty-seven enemy dead lay in front of Lachhiman's section, 31 of which lay directly in front of his trench. His comrades were in no doubt that the rifleman had saved them all, for had the Japanese overrun his position then the reverse slope would have fallen and the whole company would have been wiped out.

Rifleman Lachhiman Gurung was evacuated to hospital but the surgeons were unable to save his right hand and the use of his right eye. He bore his wounds without complaint and after several weeks in hospital he was fit enough to return to his unit.

The Parade

And now the proudest moment in his life had arrived. The order to stand to attention was bellowed out across the parade ground and every soldier snapped to attention as if one man.

'Rifleman Lachhiman Gurung. Three paces to the front!'

The Gurkha soldier stamped his right foot and marched smartly from the ranks of his comrades, his arms swinging in wide arcs before clattering to a halt and standing stiffly to attention. The broad brim of his hat shielded his eyes from the glare of the sun as a tall British official approached him. This was no less a person than His Excellency, Field Marshall Lord Wavell, the Viceroy who ruled India on behalf of King George VI.

For a brief moment, Lachhiman glanced beyond His Excellency to where his father was sitting on the edge of the parade ground. Too old to walk the distance from his remote village in Nepal, he had been carried for eleven days to be present at the Red Fort ceremony. A small tear gathered at the corner of the old man's eye as the Viceroy pinned the Victoria Cross on his son's chest.

FIGHTING FACTS

What happened to Rifleman Lachhiman Gurung?

Despite the loss of his right hand and eye, Lachhiman continued to serve in the 8th Gurkha Rifles, remaining in India after the country became independent from Britain in 1948. He was promoted to Havildar, the equivalent of a sergeant, but then retired shortly afterwards to his village in Nepal. The tradition of his family serving in the army, however, lived on. To the great pride of his father, Lachhiman's son also enlisted in the 8th Gurkha Rifles, eventually rising to the rank of officer.

Strengths of British and Japanese units in Burma
British

Army	60,000–100,000
Corps	30,000–50,000 (an army has three corps)
Infantry division	13,700 (a corps has three divisions)
Infantry brigade	2,500 (a division has three brigades)
Infantry company	127 (a battalion has four companies)
Infantry platoon	32 (a company has three platoons)
Infantry section	8 (a platoon has three sections)

A British division's battalions would be entirely British troops. In an Indian division, a third would be British, the rest Indians and Gurkhas.

Japanese
The Japanese division in Burma varied greatly in strength, between 12,000 and 22,000. In total their troops varied between 100,000–120,000.

From All Over the Empire
It is sometimes forgotten that millions of soldiers from India, Pakistan, Bangladesh, Africa and the Caribbean also fought alongside British troops. In World War II around three million people from the Indian sub-conti-

nent joined the Allied war effort, forming the largest volunteer army the world has ever seen. Of the 27 Victoria Crosses awarded during the Burma campaign, members of the Indian armed services won 20. Several thousand people from the Caribbean also served, as did 375,000 Africans.

At last they are to be recognized. A set of commemorative gates will be set up in the near future near to Buckingham Palace – as a constant reminder of their bravery and sacrifice.

Orde Wingate

Orde Wingate was a British soldier who had first made a name for himself leading Jewish fighters against Arab rebels in Palestine in 1936. He put forward the idea of sending forces deep behind Japanese lines so that they could launch unexpected attacks. His guerrilla soldiers were called 'Chindits' and the first force of 3,000 proved so successful that his army was expanded to 12,000.

They were kept supplied from airdrops but if any were wounded they had to be left behind and take their luck in being captured. Wingate himself was killed in an air crash on 24 March 1944.

Not likely!

The Chindits would disappear into the jungle for months at a time and, to prevent their families worrying, an officer was given the job of writing postcards back to their homes. The officer would write that, 'at the end of the operation he will write home as usual'. One angry mother complained bitterly. What did they mean 'as usual'? She hadn't heard from her son for three years!

GLOSSARY

Bren gun – a lightweight quick-firing machine-gun

Gurkha – a Nepalese soldier serving in the British army

Luftwaffe – the German air force

Panzer – armoured troops or a German tank

Partisan – a guerrilla fighter, loyal to a cause

PIAT (Projector Infantry anti-tank) – a hand-held anti-tank
   weapon, which at close quarters could disable a tank

Sten gun – a type of lightweight sub-machine-gun

ACKNOWLEDGEMENTS

Imperial War Museum: p.148 FX7529, p.149 LD305, p.156 E13465, p.161 E18493, p.180 MH27176, p.182 HU49815, p.188 B5013, p.190 B5114, p.193 B5055, p.203 BU1024, p.208 MH2061, p.220 HU2127, p.236 IND3479, p.237 IND3616, p.239 IB283; AKG Photo: p.183 2–G56–W3–1941–25; Robert Hunt Library: p.199, p.203 CL1169, p.209.

Every effort has been made to trace copyright holders. We would be grateful to hear from any copyright holders not acknowledged here.